The Steelers of Farrell, PA

The Inside Story of the 2018 Farrell High School Steelers Pennsylvania State Football Championship

The Steelers of Farrell, PA

The Inside Story of the 2018 Farrell High School Steelers Pennsylvania State Football Championship

by Darwin Huey

Front cover photo courtesy of Leigh O'Shane Phanco
Front cover design by Peter David Communications
Back cover photo courtesy of Clark's Studio

The Steelers of Farrell, PA
The Inside Story of the 2018 Farrell High School Steelers
Pennsylvania State Football Championship

Featuring Coach Samuels' championship season journal

The storied tradition of Farrell High School Sports

ISBN 978-1-73585594-3

Doc Publishing
P.O. Box 7503
New Castle, PA 16107

Dedication

This book is dedicated to:

The memory of Kathy Stewart (1952-2018), Farrell High School Class of 1970, the mother of Coach Jarrett Samuels, who had the 'Best Seat in the House' for the 2018 championship season; and

Janet Chisholm Shannon (1939-2020), my friend, Farrell High School Class of 1957; and

All Farrell Steelers—past, present, and future.

Author's Note

The deeper I researched the history of Farrell High School sports, the more my unworthiness for this task was unveiled. I couldn't help but venture beyond this exciting football championship season into the rich story of the Steelers of Farrell. Then, I quickly realized that a comprehensive book was not possible. But a brief peek behind the numerous championship banners displayed in McCluskey Gym was tantalizing.

So, as you proceed, know that for any of my literary passes that are intercepted, any of my grammatical fumbles, any factual mistakes…I tug the front of my jersey to indicate the fault is mine and mine alone.

I was inspired by these words written in 1990 by the venerable Ray Swanson in his Keystoner column in the *Youngstown Vindicator:*

"What's the secret to Farrell's success? The secret is pride, tradition, and excellent coaching. The odds have been stacked against Farrell for years due to its small size. Still Steeler teams continue to raise the eyebrows of Pennsylvania sports fans. It's a tribute to the players, coaches, and the school. As long as there's Farrell, there's something to root for in the world of scholastic sports."

Contents

Foreword

There is often talk about taking a trip down Memory Lane. This book, *The Steelers of Farrell, PA*, not only takes me back to the memories of Farrell High School State Football Championships, but also to so much more.

I have been blessed to sit mic-side and deliver play-by-play of so many great high school moments. Farrell has often been the subject of some of the most memorable sporting events I've ever called.

Dar Huey not only helped me re-visualize sporting events, but he also took me back to my childhood that included visiting my grandparents in Farrell or sitting in a jam-packed gymnasium with my uncle and my dad. Dar takes me back to the birthplace of my fandom, Farrell, PA, and yet again triggers the goosebumps of Farrell football's amazing State Championship success.

The Steelers of Farrell, PA gives us all a peek inside the Steel City. Just like the small roadside sign entering Farrell proclaims, "Welcome to Farrell, City of Champions".

Mark Slezak, the Keith Jackson of the Shenango Valley, the longtime voice of Mercer County high school sports and the voice of the Westminster College Titans. December 2024.

High school sports are exciting. High school teams are borne out of a deep-rooted history of toughness that is forged in the blue-collar industries by hard-working men and women.

This journal speaks right to those of us who were born in the Rust Belt where the hometown team was/is the catalyst to the city's survival.

Farrell's head coach, Jarrett Samuels, embodies the heart of his town. This is the story of a pure soul whose love for his players is unmatched and of a team that embraced his direct process and mirrored the character that he modeled. This process was about far more than winning a championship. This was about meeting kids where they are and growing them into winners through a process that will impact generations.

Ralph Blundo, Head Basketball Coach of the New Castle Red Hurricane and the subject of the book, Together: The Inside Story of the 2014 New Castle Red Hurricane Pennsylvania State AAAA Basketball Championship. In Blundo's fifteen years his Red Hurricane have won ten Section championships, seven WPIAL championships, and the 2014 State championship. December 2024.

Preface

The endeavor to write this book began in the winter of 2019. The gleam on the state championship trophy was still shining as brightly as the smile on Coach Samuels' face.

Four years earlier I had written a book, *Together: The Inside Story of the New Castle Red Hurricane 2014 Pennsylvania State Basketball Championship,* about the team which was coached by my friend and former student, Ralph Blundo.

During a routine meeting at the office of my friend and former player, Jarrett Samuels, I posed the idea of writing *The Steelers of Farrell, PA: The Inside Story of the 2018 Farrell Steelers Pennsylvania State Football Championship.* He immediately embraced the concept.

Then, unbeknownst to me, but to my delight, Jarrett told me he had kept a day-by-day journal of the season which would enable a rare inside perspective. On my next visit, he entrusted the journal to me, and the project began. His journal from pre-season camp to the state trophy celebration is embedded throughout this manuscript.

Then, two years into the project, this writer was burglarized in North Carolina. Among the thief's plundered items were the briefcase with the first drafts of this book. The thief never returned the goods, nor did he offer any editorial counsel. I hope he enjoyed the story.

Then Coach Amp Pegues, who had succeeded Coach Samuels, just went ahead and led the Steelers to their second consecutive state championship. That matched Coach Lou Falconi's 1995 and 1996 back-to-back state titles. Incidentally, the 1995 Steelers were quarterbacked by Amp Pegues. So that deserved an epilogue here.

Then, for the next three years, the coronavirus rocked the world and continued to rock it. This tragic worldwide event limited access to people, places, and resources and consequently, further delayed the progress of this project.

It was sort of like getting thrown for a loss, then called for a delay of game penalty, and then being charged with a COVID personal foul.

So, here it is, later than expected, but pleased to share it. While it was my pen that was put to paper, it was the performance of the skilled players, the preparation of the coaches, and the spirit of the Farrell community that wrote this story.

In the aftermath of the celebration on December 6, 2018, at Hersheypark Stadium, Coach Samuels told a reporter… "If I wrote a book, it would have a great ending!"

Well, you know the ending! Here is the book.

Chapter One

The Steel City...
City of Champions

"...the most dominant team in Mercer County History..."

"If you like underdog stories this is NOT one."

Chapter One

The Steel City...
City of Champions

This is a story about the Steel City, this is the story about the City of Champions. Anyone who enters the city limits of Farrell, PA is greeted by this blue and gold sign:

Welcome to Farrell
City of Champions
21 State Champions
Basketball – 7 Football – 2
Wrestling – 3 Girls Track – 1
Girls Volleyball – 8

There is another city notable for steel and champions. It lies 69 miles to the south and it also can lay claim to a significant history of steel production and to the title "City of Champions." But this "other" city and the "other" Steelers (and Pirates and Penguins) can boast of only 14 championships. Steelers – 6, Pirates – 3, Penguins – 5. That city is just called Pittsburgh.

On Thursday, December 6, 2018, the Farrell High School Football Steelers rendered the "Welcome to Farrell" signs inaccurate. For it was on this day at Hersheypark Stadium that those Steelers put their team in the record books. And they put their signature on those signs for posterity to remember the most dominant football team in Mercer County history, as the county's only undefeated state champions.

Since the inception of the state playoffs in 1988, there have been 130 champions crowned in all classifications. Only eleven have come from District 10 and only five from Mercer County. Hickory 1989 (2A), Sharpsville 1997 (1A), and Farrell 1995, 1996, 2018 (1A).

If you like underdog stories, this is NOT one. These Farrell High School Steelers were the New York Yankees of the 1920s, Murderer's Row with Babe Ruth...they were the Chicago Bears, Monsters of the Midway in the 1940s...they were the dominant Boston Celtics with

Bill Russell of the 1960s. They were their own version of the "Steel Curtain" just like those "other" Steelers.

Farrell was favored from the start, ranked number one in the state even before the first kickoff of the season. They were highlighted in red on every opponent's schedule.

They methodically proceeded to go wire-to-wire, imposing the mercy rule fourteen times, thirteen times in the first half, in fifteen games.

Take a look at some of the season's numbers:

100	The one-hundredth year of Farrell football (a good time to celebrate)
15-0	Only the third undefeated team in FHS history (1940: 9-0) (1959: 8-0-2)
779-117	Outscored their opponents
616-30	Outscored their opponents in the first half
174-18	Outscored their opponents in the first half of PIAA playoff games
103	Total touchdowns
59	Touchdowns of 20+ yards
10	Defensive and special teams' touchdowns
26.5	Sacks
0	Sacks allowed
35	Takeaways (11 interceptions, 24 fumble recoveries)
6500-2438	Yards gained – yards allowed

IF

If this football team were a boxer, it would have been an onslaught of first round knockout punches. They scored 616 of their 779 points in the first half, 79% of their scoring.

If this football team were a baseball team, they would have been swinging from their heels, going for the fences. Fifty-nine touchdowns went for 20 yards or more.

If this football team were a basketball team, there would have been a barrage of rim-rattling, crowd-pleasing slam dunks... for all of the excitement that they generated.

If they were the Department of Defense, they would have been highly decorated for the shock and awe they created. In fifteen games they allowed a total of 30 points in the first halves of games.

Chapter Two

The City of Farrell

"…the population of Farrell represented a broad
cross-section of the nations."

"…the different ethnic groups meshed together in this new
society to provide the power for the engine
of the steel industry."

Chapter Two

The City of Farrell

Geography

The City of Farrell, while looming large on the landscape of high school sports in the Commonwealth, is geographically just a small city of only 2.27 square miles. It is located in Western Pennsylvania about halfway between Erie to the north and Pittsburgh to the south. The Ohio state line creates its western border which is approximately traced by the Shenango River. To the south lies the smaller Borough of Wheatland which is included within the Farrell Area School District. The larger City of Hermitage is Farrell's eastern neighbor. To the north is the City of Sharon. The area that is now Farrell was originally named the Borough of South Sharon when it was incorporated as a separate jurisdiction in 1901.

The lower or western end of the city along the Ohio border lies in the flood plain of the Shenango River. Frequent floods occurred in early years, most notably the disastrous flood of 1913 which caused major damage to the downtown of Sharon. Under the governorship of Gifford Pinchot, the Pymatuning Dam was completed in 1934.

Later, further downstream, the United States Army Corps of Engineers constructed the Shenango Dam in 1965. These two dams provided water supply and mitigated flooding problems. Martin Luther King, Jr. Boulevard (PA 718), was formerly known as Broadway Avenue, but to the locals it is "Swamp Road," an apt description for its low-lying topography.

The larger part of Farrell sits up the hill to the east. Main east-west streets are Idaho Street, once a bustling commercial corridor, Union Street, and Roemer Boulevard. The Farrell Elementary School and Farrell High School are located on Roemer. Among north-south avenues that bisect Roemer Boulevard are Stambaugh, Fruit – once known for its many churches, and Spearman.

The city is roughly framed by the triangle created by Route 718 (MLK, Jr. Blvd), Route 418 (Mercer Avenue), and Route 518 (Sharon New Castle Road).

Due to Farrell's curious irregular shape, it has 45 sides – enough to drive a geometry student crazy; a motorist, in just a few minutes, can drive into Wheatland or Hermitage or Sharon and then back into Farrell.

The colors of the street signs provide a clue to one's location. Hermitage signs are generally white lettering on a green background. If one is near Wheatland, the signs might be white on black or black on white, or maybe white on green. Sharon's signs are black lettering with a white background. Appropriately, in the City of Farrell, the signs are distinctly Farrell Steeler blue on gold.

Population

In its early years Farrell was referred to as the "Magic City." This was a reference to its "magical" and rapid growth resulting from the new and booming steel industry. The U.S. Census indicates that within the first decade of the steel industry in Farrell, the population grew to 10,190. Ten years later it had reached its peak population of 15,586.

The collapse of the steel industry in America in the 1970s set in motion a steady and precipitous half century of population decline. The 2010 Census reported 5,111 citizens.

By 2022 the population had further diminished to 4,418, a 13.5% reduction since the 2010 census. The population decline is perhaps most poignantly illustrated in the graduation statistics of Farrell High School. Janet Shannon's 1957 graduating class numbered 254…the 2018 Steelers' class counted only 44 on graduation day.

The numbers on the census charts only reflect part of the story of the rich history of ethnic and cultural diversity woven into the fabric of this tiny society.

Long before the United Nations was formed in San Francisco in 1945, the population of Farrell, PA represented a broad cross-section of the nations of the world. The promise of a new life in America and employment in the steel industry and its ancillary services was the magnet attracting them.

From central Europe came Slovaks, Hungarians, and Polish people seeking the hope in front of them while escaping the totalitarian rule behind them. Romanians, Croatians, Serbians, Macedonians, Bulgarians, and Greeks from the Balkans in southeastern Europe boarded ships with little more than a steamer trunk and a dream. Their motivations were both political and economic. A portion of these groups was a Jewish population fleeing from persecution. Western Europe was represented by farmers, artisans, laborers, and shopkeepers from England, Ireland, Wales, Germany, and Italy.

America's Great Migration caused the movement of millions of African-Americans from the rural south to the industrial north. The impetus for the movement was economic opportunity and escape from the racist policies and practices of Jim Crow laws which mandated segregation. The route to Farrell for most of them originated in the states of South Carolina, Virginia, Alabama, and Georgia. They provided manpower for the mills and completed the religious, racial, cultural, and ethnic diversity of the mosaic that is Farrell. Today the population is almost equally divided between Black and White citizens.

Churches

Farrell has long been known for its many churches representing a wide range of traditions. Houses of worship met spiritual needs by providing familiarity in language, liturgy, and traditions.

Some examples of historic churches with their descriptive and colorful names and identities:

• Holy Trinity Slovak Evangelical Lutheran
• Holy Cross Romanian Orthodox
• Magyar (Hungarian) Presbyterian
• St. Anthony American Croatian Roman Catholic

- St. George's Serbian Orthodox
- Greater Morris Chapel African Methodist Episcopal
- St. Adalbert's Polish Roman Catholic
- Orthodox B'Nai Zion
- Greek Orthodox Church of Annunciation
- St. Anthony de Padua Italian

While some ethnic, orthodox, and Catholic churches remain today, now the predominant churches are of the Baptist, evangelical, holiness, and pentecostal traditions.

Clubs and Homes

There existed, and still exists today to some degree, a rich history of clubs or homes which corresponded with each ethnic group. The clubs served the purpose of maintaining the culture, traditions, and language of the homeland. Italians could enjoy pasta at the Italian Home and Germans could partake of bratwurst and beer at the German Home. Young Slovaks could learn the language from older immigrant club members at the First Slovak Workingmen's Educational Club. The Romanian Home provided a cultural shelter for those from Transylvania. A member of the Croatian American Civic Club could play basketball or enjoy some crni risotto (black risotto). At the Serbian Home, slava feasts were enjoyed as each family celebrated its patron saint.

No account of this city would be complete without the acknowledgement of the role of the Twin City Elks Lodge in the social lives of the African American community. It was widely acclaimed throughout the eastern and midwestern states. Particularly noteworthy are the entertainers that the Lodge booked. During the Age of Jazz, Cab Calloway, Duke Ellington, and Louis "Satchmo" Armstrong performed on the Twin City Elks stage. On another occasion the tap dancing of "Pegleg" Bates appeared in Farrell. Ray Charles, The Temptations and the Four Tops brought soul, rhythm and blues, and the Motown sounds to the Shenango Valley. The Lodge was sort of a Cotton Club west and a Motown east. To add to the roster of famous visitors, Jesse Owens and Satchel Paige visited and signed autographs, the latter offering his signature from his signature rocking chair.

The clubs and homes played an important role in the lives of both foreign immigrants and the African-Americans from the South as they assimilated to their new lives in America's industrial north. They provided dancing, drinking, entertainment, sports, and nightlife.

In this city, there was a cacophony of many languages, dialects, and accents. An astute person could identify a person's nationality by his/her often multi-syllabic surname or by the strange sound of their languages.

Regardless, if they arrived in Farrell after the grueling trans-Atlantic ship voyage or if they arrived via the challenging train ride from the South…regardless that they spoke different languages…regardless that they bore distinctly different names…the different ethnic groups meshed together in this new society to provide the power for the engine of the steel industry.

Steel

The team nickname of Farrell High School – Steelers – is transparently obvious. It can accurately be said that steel built the city. The eponymous name given to the city honors James A. Farrell who was the president of US Steel from 1911-1932. US Steel was America's first billion-dollar company.

Old timers in Farrell remember the steel industry by many different and historic names:

• Buhl Steel Company
• American Steel and Wire Company
• South Sharon Works of the American Sheet and Tin Plate Company
• US Steel Corporation
• Carnegie – Illinois Steel – Farrell Works
• Sharon Steel Hoop
• Carnegie Steel
• Sharon Steel
• NLMK

Farrell High School sits on Roemer Avenue which takes its name from Henry Roemer, a prominent business leader and president of Sharon Steel from 1931-1957. His significant legacy to the city was shepherding the company from $500,000 in losses in 1931 to $10,000,000 in revenue by 1957. He is credited with saving the industry in Farrell.

Residents recall the fiery red night sky illuminated by the blast furnaces. Youngsters remember the glow from the cinder pits and the clinkers that simmered in the slag dump. Indicators that the steel industry was running hot. It is not possible to underestimate the significant influence of steel in this steel city.

People

In addition to the famous personalities that visited or were rumored to have visited the Twin City Elks over the years, many notable figures made their way to the city.

The most significant was then presidential candidate John F. Kennedy's campaign stop on October 15, 1960. Presidential candidate Jesse Jackson made a similar visit in 1983. Pittsburgh Steeler Lynn Swann made a visit during his gubernatorial campaign in 2006.

It is rumored that the infamous outlaw John Dillinger might have robbed the bank on Broadway Avenue. That would be just one of his 24 heists in the 1930s.

A more honorable visit was that of the famous American painter, Norman Rockwell. In the spring of 1966, Rockwell added an important series of illustrations to his gallery of Americana.

Commissioned by the Sharon Steel Corporation, in fifteen illustrations he depicted the critical steps in the manufacture of steel entitled, "The Men and Machines of Modern Steelmaking." It is said that Rockwell was impressed with "the unusual dedication of purpose" of the workers in Farrell.

Civil Rights leader and president of the National Urban League, Whitney Young, promoted his mission in Farrell.

The people of the steel industry have left a lasting mark on the city. Of course, the city itself is named after James Farrell (president of U.S. Steel), Pargny Street got its name from E.W. Pargny (president of American Sheet and Tin Plate), Roemer Blvd (Henry Roemer of Sharon Steel), and Buhl Terrace (Frank Buhl of Buhl Steel).

Some notable Farrell natives, other than football and basketball players included:

• Billy Soose, Middleweight boxing champion
• Leo Yankevich, poet
• Dr. Clarice Flint Ford, college administrator
• Bill Cardille, "Chilly Billy"
• Neal Russo, St. Louis Post – Dispatch sportswriter
• Jerry Sharell, music producer, Hollywood personality

(E.L) Elaine Lobl Konigsburg shared the distinction with basketball great Jack Marin (1962) as the valedictorian of her 1947 Farrell class. E.L. was one of only six authors to win two Newbery Awards, the highest honor by the American Library Association for distinguished contributions to children's literature. Her two winning books were *"From the Mixed-Up Files of* Mrs. Basil E. Frankweiler" (1968) and *"The View from Saturday"* (1997).

Ted Pedas was an internationally known astronomer, educator, and philanthropist. In 2001, he was honored with the City of Farrell Centurion Award. The planetarium at Farrell High School is named in his honor. He is unrivaled in his contributions to the school and the community.

Roland Barksdale-Hall has added depth and breadth to the understanding of Farrell and its history and culture in his two *Images of America* books.

Of course, that is just a snapshot. There are war heroes, priests and pastors, laborers and professional people, parents and neighbors who also define the uniqueness of Farrell.

Chapter Three

The Four Horsemen

"Outlined against the autumn skies of Western PA in 2018, the Four Horsemen rode yet again. Here they were known as Wright, Lewis, Townsend, and Hilton."

"It was their leadership, maturity, and scholarship that forged the path for this team…"

Chapter Three

The Four Horsemen

In the sixth chapter of the Book of Revelation, John wrote about the apocalyptic vision of the four horsemen, symbolizing Famine, Pestilence, Destruction, and Death…predictors of the last judgment.

Seated in the press box of the Polo Grounds on October 18, 1924, the fabled sportswriter, Grantland Rice, pounded out these inspired words from his Underwood typewriter:

"Outlined against a blue-gray October sky, the Four Horsemen rode again. In dramatic lore they are known as Famine, Pestilence, Destruction, and Death. These are only aliases. Their real names are Stuhldreher, Miller, Crowley, and Layden."

Those were the historic words of the lede on his account as the Fighting Irish of Notre Dame defeated the vaunted Army squad 12-7 on the previous day.

Outlined against the autumn skies of western PA in 2018, the Four Horsemen rode yet again. Here they were known as Wright, Lewis, Townsend, and Hilton. No need for aliases here because everyone knew exactly who they were. When the state championship trophy was hoisted in Hersheypark Stadium at season's end, it could be said that each of their fifteen opponents experienced an apocalyptic event at the hands of the Farrell Steelers.

In the game program they were listed as #1 Christian Lewis, #2 Kyi Wright, #5 Jourdan Townsend, and #57 Kobe Hilton. All four would earn first team All-State recognition. All four would earn Division I football scholarships. All four would accumulate staggering measurable statistics.

One is reminded of the words of great physics "coach" Albert Einstein who said, "Not everything that can be counted counts and not everything that counts can be counted."

While the measurables, the statistics, of the four horsemen were countable and impressive, it is the immeasurable that best define them. It was their leadership, maturity, and scholarship that forged the path for this team as much as it was their considerable and unique physical skills.

Kyi Wright

Legendary Westminster College football coach, Dr. Harold Burry, believed that every good football team had to be led at quarterback by a swashbuckler, that heroic protagonist from European adventure literature characterized by courage, daring, and skill. As for Kyi Wright, it was obvious as early as his freshmen year that his buckle could really swash.

As a 14-year-old freshman, he started at tight end and linebacker on Farrell's 14-2 PA western championship team. Max Prep named him a freshman All American. As a sophomore he played quarterback and linebacker. Before his junior season he suffered a torn medial collateral ligament in a summer AAU basketball game, causing him to miss his junior seasons in both football and basketball.

One of the enduring images of the season was that of #2, #57, #1, and #5… hands clasped and held high above their helmets…striding confidently to mid-field for the coin toss.

The Four Horsemen were prepared to ride.

As a senior, Kyi returned to the field at the quarterback position while continuing his stellar play at linebacker. On the decision to play him at quarterback, before the season began, Coach Samuels said, "Kyi gives us the best chance to win a state championship at quarterback. His experience and ability to lead a team makes it easy to put him in charge of everything. He's our best overall player."

Four months later those words would prove prophetic. The irony of this record-setting quarterback who quarterbacked his team to the championship is, he was not really a quarterback. But as he said in the preseason, "I'm very excited to get back under center to lead the offense.

It's key for us to not turn the ball over. The more we have the ball, the more damage we can do."

That would prove to be the second pre-season prophetic statement. They did not turn it over and damage they DID do!

It was his spirited leadership, his competitive fire, and his selfless desire to contribute whatever necessary to help his team win that made him the ideal field general. His excellent decision-making, superb passing accuracy, and fearless rumbling ball carrying brought delight to the Farrell fans. As a linebacker those occasions when he dropped his calling card with a crunching tackle on opposing ball carriers brought only further delight.

Kyi's leadership and athleticism also extended to the basketball court where he led the round ball Steelers to the district championship. He completed his basketball career with 1,171 points in just three seasons which ranks him ninth all time in the storied history of Farrell High School basketball. To his All-State football honors, he added a third team All-State selection in basketball.

He takes his place alongside Julius McCoy, Don Jones, Brian Generalovich, Willie Somerset, Randy Crowder, Pete Hall, and Lorenzo Styles as Farrell Steelers who combined gridiron and hardcourt excellence.

During this championship season, Kyi accounted for 2,399 total yards, and 45 touchdowns. His season passing numbers: 19 touchdowns, 1,671 yards, 70.3% completion percentage, and only two interceptions.

The spirited, talented, articulate, confident Kyi Wright wrote an impressive chapter in the annals of Farrell Steeler history that will not soon be forgotten.

Jourdan Townsend

Jourdan Townsend wore the number 5 on his blue and gold jersey. The PIAA state record book wears many numbers for pass receiving that he rang up like the stock ticker during his high school career.

He holds the state record for all classifications for career receiving touchdowns with 58. His 3,580 career receiving yards rank fourth on the all-time list and his 187 career receptions rank seventh. He owns two of the top five touchdown receptions in a season, 25 in 2018 and 22 in 2017. His 1,531 receiving yards in 2017 ranks him ninth in the state record book. So, you could say number 5 makes six appearances among the state's elite receivers. All of those statistics are reduced because of the numerous mercy rule shortened games.

On the homefront, Jourdan is Farrell High School's all-time leader in receptions (187), receiving yards (3,590), and scoring. His 75 touchdowns include 58 receiving, ten punt returns, and seven rushing.

It can easily be understood that he also holds several District 10 season and career records.

The aforementioned statistical summary frames just the quantifiable elements of Jourdan's resumé. Equally impressive are the immeasurable attributes that he brought to the team. Any mention of his individual records (some of which he wasn't even aware) caused him to defer to the team. He displayed that greatest quality of any team sport athlete - he was a good teammate.

Before the season began in an interview with WYTV he said, "We just want to bring the championship back in the 100-year anniversary of the football team, that would be the icing on the cake. Growing up together this has been a dream for us."

Notice the emphasis on "we," "together" and "us."

He combined his mature confidence with a fierce competitiveness. An old retired football coach who had been scouting players for a half century thought that Jourdan had the finest set of hands of any high school receiver that he had ever seen. He nestled the ball as if nurturing a wounded bird, then clamped on it with the grip of a blacksmith.

Farrell Steeler fans will long remember the acrobatic catches, the explosive kick returns, the game-changing plays, and the leadership of number 5, Jourdan Townsend...the receiving horse of the Four Horsemen.

Christian Lewis

When Christian Lewis pulled his #1 jersey over his shoulder pads, the singular blue numeral on his jersey cut an image of a well-dressed, dignified gentleman wearing a tie on his way to church. It wasn't just an image. He is a gentleman and he is familiar with the entrance to the church as well as the entrance to the end zone.

Christian played the game befitting that image. In the championship season (#1 team) he became Farrell's all-time leading rusher (#1 rusher). He earned Regional Player of the Year recognition (#1 player) and All-State honors.

During his senior year, Christian rushed for 2,466 yards and scored 38 touchdowns. In the four PIAA playoff games he scored thirteen touchdowns. On the biggest stage under the brightest lights in the state championship game, #1 capped the season with five touchdowns and 249 rushing yards.

Christian could run past defenders with his sprinter speed (state qualifier in the 100 and 200). His explosiveness enabled him to burst around them. With his power, he ran over them when necessary. His B-button spin move was executed at full speed and a sight to behold. A sight that many would-be tacklers never beheld.

His God-given talent combined with his considerable work ethic created a running back who could cut, slither, spin, swerve, accelerate, and score...and score some more.

The character and dignity and humility of Christian was best illustrated by his touchdown "celebration." It consisted of handing the ball to the official or setting the ball down in the end zone and returning to the bench. Not an ounce of hot dog in him.

In a WYTV-TV interview during pre-season camp, Christian said, "The sky is the limit for us… It's crazy… We have a chance to do something special." The history books will record what they did.

The soft-spoken running back let his actions speak loudly. No player created more excitement than the classy guy with the #1 on his jersey.

Kobe Hilton

When Kobe Hilton took his position, he interrupted the skyline of the line of scrimmage. His presence approximated an image, not unlike a smokestack at Sharon Steel. It might be called Tower 57. Beneath that tower was the blast furnace that blazed hot with the fires of competition.

Every opponent's scouting report paid particular attention to number 57. The difficulty was locating him. He may have been aligned at any position along the offensive or defensive line. And what a sight it was to behold when he stationed his 6'5, 282-pound body in the backfield. One can imagine the size of the eyes and the trembling in the hearts of the defenders as they considered the prospects of taking on the behemoth at blocking back. Some certainly decided pre-snap to make a business decision.

A testament to his durability, he started all 58 games of his high school career…to his versatility, he played as many as seven positions …to his athleticism, he also excelled in basketball, volleyball, and track and field.

Most football coaches would value strength and size in their linemen. It would be an additional bonus to combine athleticism, agility, and competitive spirit. Kobe was that rare package in a high school lineman.

Of course, few statistics are recorded for linemen but the phenomenal statistics compiled by Christian, Kyi, and Jourdan were made possible by the performance of Heart and Soul and their leader, Kobe Hilton.

The Farrell Steelers had Kobe Hilton. Number 57 in the program and on the smokestack and in the blast furnace.

The Four Horsemen in the Fall of 2023

As this book went to the press five years after the state championship, the Four Horsemen were still mounted on their steeds and taking advantage of redshirts and the additional year of eligibility granted by the NCAA due to the COVID pandemic.

Christian Lewis

After four seasons as a defensive back and kick returner with the University of Albany Great Danes, Christian took his degree in Homeland Security and enrolled at Austin Peay University as a graduate student. Christian played cornerback for the Governors who went 9-3 in the Fall of '23 and earned a national playoff spot.

Jourdan Townsend

Jourdan also took advantage of the COVID ruling and played the 2023 season (his fifth year) for the Blue Hens of the University of Delaware. His team's 9-4 record qualified for the national playoffs. Jourdan completed his collegiate career as one of Delaware's all-time leading receivers along with a sterling academic record.

Kobe Hilton

Kobe also extended his career with the Miami (OH) Redhawks as a defensive lineman. Taking advantage of the redshirt year and the COVID year, Kobe still has another season of eligibility in 2024. In 2023 Miami went 11-3 and earned an invitation to the Cure Bowl.

Kyi Wright

After three years with the Pitt Panthers, Kyi transferred to James Madison University. As a tight end for the Dukes, he still has another year of eligibility in 2024. James Madison finished the season 11-2 and played in the Armed Forces Bowl.

So, the Four Horsemen were still playing and still winning in 2023…a combined record of 40-12 and all four teams earned postseason berths. More importantly, all four had earned bachelor's degrees and continued on to earn second degrees or master's degrees.

Seniors

In addition to the Four Horsemen, seven more seniors contributed their leadership and unique skills to this magical season.

#3 Elijah Harper - WR, S

Known as "Playboi"
- Stabilizing influence as the centerfielder of the defense.
- Bespectacled safetyman
- Pound for pound as tough as anyone
- Intercepted pass in western final with broken hand

#7 Natoreaus Atwood – RB, OLB

- Hustler
- Positive influence
- Leading tackler
- Special teams leader
- Missed season - August 14 non-contact knee injury

#8 Everton Rawlins - WR, CB

- Selfless teammate
- Competitive
- Blocker

#22 Tymir Green - FB, MLB

- Tough, rugged, both sides of the ball
- Enforcer
- Gritty - played through ankle injury

#25 Cameron Zimmerman - RB, OLB

- Jourdan and Christian encouraged him to play
- Accepted his role without complaint
- Good teammate

#50 Vincent Purdy - OL, DL

- Dedicated program kid
- Practiced hard
- All four years

#58 Dashon Sims - OL, DL

- Intense
- Emotional
- Hard nosed
- Hit of the year in championship game
- "Big Hurt"

Chapter Four

The Regular Season

Mercy! Mercy!

"100 years of Farrell football!"

"...this season could be magical"
(from Coach Samuels' journal)

Chapter Four

The Regular Season

Scouting Report for Readers

Each game has three components.

1. **Jarrett's Journal** - Example: "Jarrett's Journal - University Prep - Week #1." This segment is Coach Samuel's daily journal (Monday-Thursday) of preparation and reflection.

2. **Game Report** - Example: "University Prep-Game Report." This segment is the author's reportage after each game.

3. **Jarrett's Game Day Journal** - Example: "Jarrett's Game Day Journal - University Prep." This segment features Jarrett's Game Day (Friday) reflections.

This pattern is then repeated for every game of the season.

Jarrett's Journal - Pre-season

M Aug 6

- First day of acclimatization
- Thinking our numbers look great
- Time to make this season special

M Aug 13

- First day of double sessions. Bittersweet
- Thinking this is my seniors last high school camp ever
- Kyi, Crit, JT, Kobe, Vinny, Playboi, Big Hurt, Everton, Tymir, Natoreus, Newcomer-Zim

T Aug 14

- My Glue Guy, special teams phenom, starting linebacker Natoreus goes down, non-contact injury
- Wow! Another senior season cut short
- Thinking/hoping it's not bad
- This kid is the ultimate hustle player, optimistic

S Aug 18

- First scrimmage
- A success, looked good
- No injuries

Jarrett's Journal - University Prep - Week #1

M Aug 20

• 4 goals: Region I Champs, District 10 Champs, Western Final Champs, State Champs, Undefeated - a Bonus

T Aug 21

• Team mantra - HUSTLE!!!

W Aug 22

• Great week of preparation
• Everyone excited about first game

R Aug 23

• 100 years of Farrell football - wow!
• This season could be magical
• One for the ages
• All of the omens are in place

University Prep Game Report

The Farrell Steelers prepared for the opening kickoff of the school's one hundredth season as the number one ranked single "A" team in the Commonwealth by the *Harrisburg Patriot News.*

While it would be a demanding challenge to maintain that early recognition, the prognosticators would prove prescient as the season unfolded. This group of Steelers was confident and focused; they boldly and unapologetically proclaimed that the state championship that had eluded them the past three years was their goal. Their bumper sticker read "State Championship or Bust!"

The season opened on a muggy August 24 night at Cupples Stadium in Pittsburgh, that other City of Champions. Their opponent, the University Prep Wildcats, was determined to schedule a challenging non-conference opponent to prepare them for Pittsburgh City League play.

University Prep, located in the Hill District of Pittsburgh, is a partnership between the University of Pittsburgh and the Pittsburgh Public Schools. The Wildcats are coached by Louis Berry, Jr, who was an outstanding cornerback for the Westminster College Titans where he was a team captain and two-time national champion. Coach Berry and Coach Samuels were teammates at Westminster for one year. Lou aided Jarrett's transition to college and to college football as his mentor and 'big brother.' Importantly, two decades later, they remain good friends. This was a classic brother v. brother contest.

The Steelers script that was written on opening night was to be repeated all season long. Its outline read like this… 1) Fast starts 2) Big plays 3) Mercy rule. Farrell led 40-0 before Prep scored 16 points in the fourth quarter.

Kyi completed 11 of 14 passes for 173 yards and two touchdowns. Christian rushed for 155 yards and Jourdan caught nine passes for 146 yards and two touchdowns. Brian Hilton Jr.'s four extra point conversions would be a harbinger of his season of kicking proficiency.

The final score was 40-16. Coach Berry got the tough opponent he had hoped for. The warm postgame embrace between Coach Samuels and Coach Berry was a symbol of sportsmanship, friendship, and the unbreakable and undeniable bond of Titans.

Jarrett's Game Day Journal - University Prep

F Aug 24

- Pregame - my college brother Lou Berry - UP head coach
- Brotherhood embrace
- Thinking heavy about my mother before pre-game speech
- First game ever coaching that she's not been in the stands

- Can't hear her voice anymore
- Walking sidelines, tears flowing uncontrollably
- I can't dry my face, I'm numb, standing still
- No players or coaches notice
- If they did, they never said a word
- I don't remember the first series
- I gathered myself
- My team rolls
- Upset the second team gave up 16 points
- 40-16 Farrell

Jarrett's Journal - Wilmington - Week #2

M Aug 27

- Coach O - great defensive game plan
- Must play their complicated wing – T

T Aug 28

- Bad practice

W Aug 29

- Bad practice
- Need someone to lead

R Aug 30

- Another bad practice
- One day before showdown with #2 Double A team in state
- Thinking, we are in trouble, my guys better wake up or we will be humbled in front of a large crowd
- Remembered Coach Huey saying use timeout to break momentum

Wilmington Game Report

The second week of the season pitted two of the best teams in the state against each other. Probably the premier matchup in the state on this last day of August. Wilmington and Farrell are separated by just eight miles but they are much closer than that in rich football traditions. It was the Steelers first opportunity to showcase themselves before the large home crowd on the natural grass of Lou Falconi Field at Anthony J. Paulekas Stadium. The much-anticipated contest between the #2 ranked 2A Greyhounds against the #1 ranked 1A Steelers proved to be the battle that was expected.

The first quarter featured the Hounds All-State running back Cameron Marrett breaking loose on two buck sweeps for touchdown runs of 35 and 44 yards to put Wilmington in the lead 12-0.

It marked the first time the Steelers had fallen behind in this young season. They would find themselves trailing only two more times the rest of the season, after the first series of the Western Final and after the first series of the State Championship game.

It was the second consecutive game in which classy young coaches, fellow Westminster graduates and friends, faced each other. Coach Samuels and Greyhound coach Brandon Phillian were both charged with carrying the torch of their respective programs, succeeding two of Pennsylvania's winningest coaches, Farrell's Lou Falconi and Wilmington's Terry Verrelli. Falconi and Verrelli combined for 68 years and 510 victories. At season end both Samuels and Phillian would be named Pennsylvania Coach-of-the-Year in their respective classifications.

Both coaches embraced a vision of football that extends far beyond the goalposts of the gridiron. They are cognizant that the true measure of their players' successes will be measured on other fields on other days. On fields where there will be no scoreboards.

.

After this hotly contested battle, both coaches agreed that this game was important for their teams' development in this season that would conclude for both at Hersheypark Stadium in the first week of December.

The Steelers withstood the Greyhounds early surge and countered with a Lewis touchdown at 5:42 of the second quarter and a Wright pass to a diving Townsend with just 7.8 seconds left in the half to tie the score at 12-12.

The second half began with a fortuitous set of "threes." The Hounds started the second half from their own three-yard line and then fumbled the ball away three plays later. Then three plays later Kyi's pass to Brian Hilton Jr. put the Steelers up 18-12. Then yet another three. Three plays later Farrell forced a Wilmington punt, that despite their efforts to keep the ball away from the dangerous Townsend, that settled into Jourdan's hands. What followed was a scintillating back-breaking 64-yard return for a touchdown. Score 24-12.

The defense continued to thwart the Hounds vaunted Delaware Wing-T attack. Then in the fourth quarter, Tyree Hammonds returned an interception to the one yard-line, Kyi then bulled into the endzone to make the final score 30-12. That would prove to be the only non-mercy rule game of the season and the only game in which Farrell was outgained, 293-180.

The keys to victory for the season were established:

• Field position
• Big plays
• Poise
• Resolve
• Turnover margin 3-1

It was a sweet victory for Coach Samuels. He still felt the sting of the then junior linebacker whose Steelers lost to Wilmington 10-7 in the 1989 WPIAL Championship game.

After the game a disappointed but classy Coach Phillian said, "I give Farrell credit, Coach Samuels and his players; they won the game, they made the key plays when they had to. I tip my hat to them. They are a good team."

Jarrett's Game Day Journal - Wilmington

F Aug 31

• Game day - sold out
• #1 IA Team v. #2 2A Team
• pre -game speech horrible
• Ended chanting childhood song
  "We are Steelers"
• We started flat

- Defense not playing scheme, not tackling
- Down early 12-0
- Remembered Coach Huey saying use timeouts to break momentum
- During timeouts looking at my team…talking to them
- There's no picnic, no fear
- Thinking we are down, but we played terrible
- Then boom! We hit the switch
- Flurry and tie them 12-12 at half
- Told guys, we got them, they're tired
- Second half - we dominate 31-19 (2-0)

Jarrett's Journal - Union City Week #3

M Sept 3

- Feeling great inside knowing that Wilmington was the best team we will face all season
- At that moment I know, if we stay healthy, we will win the state title
- Told the seniors we need to practice better going forward

T Sept 4

- New practice format, more competitive to liven' up practice
- Competition in every drill, we have to keep the fire
- Live drills without guys getting hurt

W Sept 5

- Freshman Anthony Jackson had a great game against Wilmington, told Coach O we found a diamond in the rough
- Jackson's role will be bigger, Natoreus' ACL is torn, out for the season – damn

R Sept 6

- Thinking things are going great, now I'm distracted by things that have nothing to do with football
- Just ignoring everything that I feel is not supporting my program

Union City Game Report

The third game of the season was a game of big numbers. It was the 1000th game in the history of Farrell High School football. The guys decided to celebrate the occasion with a touchdown scoring party. Kyi passed to Jourdan for touchdowns of 19, 4, 11, 14, and 69 yards.

Christian added touchdown runs of 10 and 16 yards. Jaden Harrison scored from 10 yards and Anthony Jackson returned a kickoff

60 yards for another. Carlos Daniels added the last touchdown from 24 yards. The big numbers included 497 yards of total offense and a final score of 70-6.

Jarrett's Game Day Journal - Union City

F Sept 7

- Game 3 - Union City
- Laser focus
- Walking on the field, I'm hearing mom's voice
- Emotional pre-game speech, feel mom's presence
- We dominate all phases
- Oh Yeah! We are good

Jarrett's Journal - West Middlesex Week #4

M Sept 10

• Rivalry week

T Sept 11

• My team is upset with me
• "Coach, these guys are not our rivals!"
• My reply, "Well smash them then!"

W Sept 12

• Lack of focus
• Team too jovial during practice
• They know my juices flow hard for this game

R Sept 13

• Juju's 17th birthday
• Good film study

West Middlesex Game Report

Just 30 seconds into the game against their Region I rival, Christian Lewis broke free on a 40-yard scoring jaunt. It sounded the beginning of a familiar refrain, "Lewis, Wright, Townsend, Lewis, Townsend, Wright." Six touchdowns plus four Hilton, Jr's PAT's.

The first half score was 34-0. The yardage advantage for the game was 367 to 96.

No account for this team or this season would be complete without honoring the "Heart and Soul". Everyone in the Farrell program acknowledged that the fireworks that the Four Horsemen ignited were made possible by the efforts of "Heart and Soul" - the Steelers offensive line.

Left Tackle - Kobe Hilton
Left Guard - Melvin Hobson, Jr.
Center - Gary Satterwhite III
Right Guard - Gary Hopson, Jr.
Right Tackle - Dashon Sims

Hobson replaced Ronald Lacamera Jr. who suffered a broken wrist in the Union City game.

"Heart and Soul" was aptly dubbed. They were a big, mobile, athletic group averaging 290 pounds and 6-2 ½ ... an uncommon group of size and skill for a class A high school, or any high school.

The 40-0 victory over the Big Reds marked the 105th career win for Coach Samuels which surpassed the career total of Anthony Paulekas. He now stood only behind his coach and mentor, the legendary Lou Falconi.

Ed Farrell, sportswriter for the Sharon Herald, does an excellent job of chronicling high school sports in Mercer County. He captured the humble essence of this game's star, Christian Lewis, when he wrote:

"When Christian Lewis speaks, it's virtually inaudible; when Christian Lewis carries the ball, it's with the impact of a thunderclap."

In defeat, West Middlesex rookie head coach Mark Means assessed the Steelers thusly:

"Farrell is as good as advertised, they've got speed, they've got size, their guys get off the football very well, they blocked well...my hat's off to them."

Many future opponents would attest to the accuracy of his analysis. And that was two tips of the hat, by opposition coaches, in just four weeks.

Jarrett's Game Day Journal – West Middlesex

F Sept 14

- Game day
- Coach O great pre-game speech
- Battle of unbeaten teams
- It's 70 degrees and humid
- Why is the grass ten feet tall and soaking wet
- I'm laughing inside
- They are scared
- O-Line continues to dominate
- We roll 40-0, mercy rule, baby!

Jarrett's Journal - Cambridge Springs - Week #5

S Sept 16

• We can't win state if we don't dominate up front

M Sept 17

• More bad news, Ronnie Lacamera, starting right guard, broke his hand - season ending
• Thinking how to reshuffle the deck on O-line

T Sept 18

• Good attitudes today
• Told captains to handle the freshmen - they need some tough love

W Sept 19

• Keep the train on the track

R Sept 20

• Thursday night film study
• Our focus has continued to progress
• Thanks Coach Kenneth/wife Nicole for feeding the team

Cambridge Springs Game Report

Another fast start against the Devils of Cambridge Springs - 35-0 first quarter, 43-0 halftime led to 63-0 final. The Steelers compiled 473 yards.

Christian continued his senior year explosion with 213 yards and touchdowns of 57, 59, and 37 yards. Kyi added two touchdowns. The youngsters announced their presence, freshmen Anthony Jackson scored two non-offensive touchdowns on a 25-yard fumble recovery return and a 30-yard interception return. Sophomore Jaden Harrison scored on an

8-yard run and freshman Anthony Stallworth concluded the scoring with a 40-yard run. The Steelers had now outscored their opponents 103-0 in the previous eight quarters.

Jarrett's Game Day Journal – Cambridge Springs

F Sept 21

- Game Day
- Back at home vs. Cambridge Springs
- Execute
- Continue to be disciplined in all three phases
- Keep guys healthy
- Young guys raise their level of play
- We want another donut
- Farrell rolls 63-0, 5-0

Jarrett's Journal - Mercer Week #6

M Sept 24

• Practice like champions

T Sept 25

• Sleepless nights, still mourning my mother
• Thank God for my wife, my queen Tracey. My rock. Love her

W Sept 26

• Marco Polo phone sessions with my siblings are so therapeutic for me
• Love my dynamic duo Paul and Cree

R Sept 27

• Showed up for work. Mrs. Maravala, teacher's aide, decorates my office
  in Mercer Mustang gear. Leaves a Mercer hoodie on my chair
• I'm thinking great motivation
• I put it on our football social media site
• She will regret the prank
• My guys - focused

Mercer Game Report

The Mustangs visited Lou Falconi Field on the night of Farrell High's homecoming celebration. The celebrating on this night was all Farrell blue and gold. Another fast start got the Steelers off to a 41-0 halftime lead. Jourdan had an extraordinary receiving night with nine receptions for 174 yards and three touchdowns - two from Kyi and one from Christian Hartley. Kyi also added two more rushing TD's and one more on a pick six, Christian scored on a 45-yard pass from Kyi and a ten-yard run. Final score 47-0

The stalwart defense allowed only two first downs and 75 total yards. The Mustangs pulled that hoodie over their heads and headed for home.

The Steelers season now stood at:
6-0 overall record
2-0 Region I record and held opponents scoreless for twelve straight quarters while scoring 150 points.

Jarrett's Game Day Journal - Mercer

F Sept 28

- Game Day
- No pep talk needed
- Guys used the prank for motivation
- Another donut
- Domination
- Could have scored 80
- Stay humble, stay focused
- 47-0
- Pregame coin toss - still get emotional…point to my mom and Donald in the sky

Jarrett's Journal - Cochranton Week #7

M Oct 1

- New week, new goals
- Work on all offensive plays…trick plays…Spartan package

T Oct 2

- One game at a time
- Keep your focus guys

W Oct 3

- Thinking Coach Emil's conditioning drills have paid huge dividends since June
- The guys may whine during the conditioning after practice
- But our strength is our condition

R Oct 4

- Good walk-through practice

Cochranton Game Report

In the seventh week of the season, the Steelers took the 50-mile road trip north to face the Cardinals of Cochranton. Christian disembarked from the bus and promptly made four more trips to the end zone on runs of 80, 8, 50, and a 78-yard kickoff return. Jaden Harrison added three touchdown trips of 29, 40, and 60. Rugged fullback Tymir Green scored two more and so did Jourdan.

At halftime the score was 56-0. The lights on the scoreboard read 76-12 when the final gun sounded.

Jarrett's Game Day Journal – Cochranton

F Oct 5

- Natoreus successful ACL surgery - thank God
- Upset during pre-game speech, we're told we have to leave the field early because of their senior night
- Had to rush pre-game routines
- Told my guys to use it, we played hard tonight, even the young guys
- Total team effort
- And their lights go out again

Jarrett's Journal - Reynolds Week #8

M Oct 8

• Prepping for Reynolds
• Thinking they can pose a challenge
• They seem to match up well on paper
• Our scouting reports are awesome

T Oct 9

• Good practice
• Thinking no team will beat us as long as we don't beat ourselves!

W Oct 10

• Great focus
• My coaches have done well with their areas, developing guys
• Our approach has been workman-like

R Oct 11

• Nobody's looking ahead
• Stay on the mission
• Attending Tymir's grandmother's funeral, she was a great lady. I grew up
  on the 300 block of Fruit, six houses down from her
• Prayers for the family

Reynolds Game Report

The short eleven-minute drive to Reynolds resulted in another short mercy-rule game. Christian scored three times, Jourdan once, and Tymir on a 29-yard return of a blocked punt, the fourth defensive touchdown of the season. Tymir honored his grandmother, whose funeral he had attended on the day before this game, with his best game to date and a celebration flip in the end zone after his touchdown.

The halftime score was 48-0. Brian Hilton, Jr. added the final touchdown to make the score 54-8. Jourdan surpassed 3,000 receiving yards for his career. The Steelers now stood at 3-0 as Region play concluded.

Jarrett's Game Day Journal - Reynolds

F Oct 12

- Pre-game old boss Bob G, stops by the locker room, he's an old Reynolds alum
- We look great in warm-up
- Reynold changed entire offense - goes wing-T
- We shut 'em down
- We storm out 28-0 first quarter
- Tymir blocks the punt, recovered in the end zone for TD
- Did a flip in the end zone, not mad about the penalty
- Tymir played his best game at linebacker to date

Jarrett's Journal - Greenville Week #9

S Oct 14

- Coaches meeting
- Don't be satisfied
- Let's keep hammering fundamentals

M Oct 15

- Senior night week

T Oct 16

- Wow! Where has the season gone!
- Week 9 already

W Oct 17

- All seniors will start the first series
- Watching WKBN Power Rankings
- They still have us picked #1 team in the Valley OH/PA
- A title we earned
- I feel great pride
- Thanks Chad and Ryan

R Oct 18

- Film study
- Guys getting a little overconfident
- Good film study

Greenville Game Report

October 19 was the last regular season game and the last time on the turf of Anthony Paulekas Stadium for eleven seniors, the Four Horsemen plus safety Elijah Harper, the injured Natoreus Atwood, wide receiver Everton Rawlins, fullback/linebacker Tymir Green, and linemen Cameron Zimmerman, Vincent Purdie, and Dashon Sims.

The Greenville Trojans traveled south to Farrell only to discover there was no fight in their Trojan horse. They became Farrell's ninth straight victim. Christian put a bow on his stellar senior year regular season with eight carries for 220 yards and three touchdowns. On this night he became Farrell's all-time rushing leader; his 3,230 yards surpassed Braxton Chapman's 3,067 yards. He added three more touchdowns which put his season total at eighteen. Jourdan's 35-yard TD reception gave him 49 for his career which tied him with Ziyon Strickland of Sharon for both the Mercer County and District 10 record.

Kyi, Tymir, and Sayvion Thomas added first half scores. The latter score a 24-yard fumble recovery return was the fifth defensive touchdown of the season.

The score at halftime was 46-0. It was the eighth first half shutout of the season, only Wilmington had scored in the first half.

No accounting of this season would be complete without a tip of the helmet to the stout and stellar defense. Defensive Coordinator Omar Stewart had erected a Steel Curtain worthy of this city's steel heritage. The defensive statistics were staggering, among them allowing only 12 points in the nine first halves of games in the regular season. The Steel Curtain lined up like this:

Defensive Ends: Brian Hilton, Jr.
Sayvion Thomas

Interior Linemen: Gary Satterwhite III
Melvin Hobson, Jr.
Kobe Hilton

Linebackers: Tymir Green
Kyi Wright
Tyree Hammonds
Anthony Jackson

Cornerbacks: Juwon Samuels
Amarion Odem

Safety: Elijah Harper

Adding poignance to this already emotional evening and only the third undefeated season in school history, was the secret action of the seniors. Unbeknownst to Coach Samuels, they had organized a fundraiser in memory of his mother. She was his inspiration and his biggest fan and the number one booster of the program. Kathy Stewart had succumbed to breast cancer on February 24. The hundreds of pink t-shirts that were sold for this night were worn in her memory…tears of sadness, tears of love.

Jarrett's Game Day Journal – Greenville

F Oct 18

- Thinking about mom all day, very emotional
- Breast Cancer Awareness game/senior night ceremony
- Seniors dedicate sales from t-shirts to cancer research in honor of my mom
- I'm overcome with emotion
- So thankful for a great bunch of seniors
- Defense almost gets scored on in first series
- Sloppy start on offense, but we get our footing - another dominant game 40-0
- Send seniors out right - perfect season 9-0
- Region I champs - #1 team in the state

The Centennial Season of Farrell High School Football

1918-2018

The Regular Season...Mercy! Mercy!

August 24 @ University Prep 40-16

August 31 Wilmington 31-19

September 7 @ Union City 70-6

September 14 @ West Middlesex 40-0

September 21 Cambridge Springs 63-0

September 28 Mercer 47-0

October 5 @ Cochranton 76-12

October 12 @ Reynolds 54-8

October 19 Greenville 46-0

Chapter 5

Destiny... The Playoffs

District 10
PIAA

Chapter 5

Destiny... The Playoffs

Jarrett's Journal – Bye Week

M Oct 22

- Bye Week
- Thinking our flow will be compromised and our rhythm will be off
- I hate Bye Weeks

T Oct 23

- JT goes down awkwardly competing in 7 on 7 drill
- I'm terrible; a major leg injury?
- Ankle swollen to football size
- JT out indefinitely
- Damn, so upset, non-contact

W Oct 24

- Trainer Dan informs me the injury is not season-ending
- Will need treatment the rest of the week
- No practice
- Thank you, Jesus. Dodged a major catastrophe

R Oct 25

- Film prep
- We are assuming Maplewood would beat Reynolds. At least I was. LOL
- I'm focusing totally on breaking down Maplewood

F Oct 26

- No game Friday as we await Reynolds vs. Maplewood winner
- At home with Tracey. We invite close friends over. Fish fry and card
  game – spades
- Lots of fun. Lots of trash talking – good night

S Oct 27

- Reynolds blows out Maplewood
- Team meeting went well

S Oct 28

- Coaches meeting. Laser focus
- Offensive and defensive preparation
- Love this part of the process
- Great film study. Game plan set

Jarrett's Journal – Reynolds
District 10 Playoffs

M Oct 29

- Excited about practice
- Found out JT still can't cut
- Captains and seniors are ready to lead

T Oct 30

- Concerned now
- JT didn't look good in drills
- Thinking he won't play Friday
- Crit will have to carry us
- Defense must be stout

W Oct 31

- So impressed by the selflessness of this team
- Especially our top guys
- No jealousy

R Nov 1

- We ready!
- Time to defend D-10 championship
- 4-peat on deck
- Told JT he may not play – ankle still a concern to me

Reynolds Game Report – District 10 Playoffs

In the tenth game of the season and the first game of District 10 playoffs, Farrell faced Region I opponent Reynolds for the second time this season, at a neutral site, Hickory High School Hornet Stadium. The Raiders entered the game with a 6-6 record coming off their 36-0 first round playoff win against Maplewood, while Farrell rested with a first-round bye. This game was played just three weeks after Farrell's 54-8 raid of the Raiders. It is said that in football it is difficult to beat a team twice in the same season. Well, that was not the case on this night. The halftime score was 48-0 which led to the final of 62-6.

Jourdan's two touchdown receptions, 49th and 50th of his career, established new Mercer County and District 10 records. Despite playing with that ankle injury, he also added another rushing TD. Christian and Tymir each accounted for two more and Kyi and Brian added one apiece.

The buzz inside Hornet Stadium was caused by another surge of big plays – touchdown passes of 23 and 48 yards and touchdown runs of 71, 39, and 34. The Steelers mounted four one play scoring "drives" and one two play "drive".

Now it was on to the District 10 championship game for the fourth consecutive year.

Jarrett's Game Day Journal – Reynolds
District 10 Playoffs

F Nov 2

- Pre-game interview on WKBN
- I missed JT in warm-ups!
- Told Bob Greenburg, WPIC game analyst, JT won't start
- But we ready
- A little nervous, worried about being out of rhythm
- Amp convinces me JT is good
- I trust him
- JT has huge game
- O-Line dominant
- Crit dominant
- Tymir – stud on defense
- Kyi – born leader
- Kobe – best D-lineman in state
- Great team effort…No rust
- We roll 62-6

Jarrett's Journal – West Middlesex
District 10 Championship

M Nov 5

- West Middlesex Round #2!
- D-10 championship at stake
- 4-Peat on the line, school record

T Nov 6

- Telling coaches West Middlesex is playing with lots of confidence
- They believe
- But we are better

W Nov 7

- Good practice
- During film study we challenge Kobe to be the dominant force on defense

R Nov 8

- Good practice
- Thinking I'm ready to play these guys Friday
- I hate Saturday games

F Nov 9

- Great walk through
- We ready
- The champs are here

West Middlesex Game Report – District 10 Championship

In a rare Saturday game, the Steelers faced the Big Red for the second time with a chance to become the first ever "4-peat" District 10 champions. After the week #4 shutout by Farrell, West Middlesex rallied to compile a 9-2 record.

The Big Red record would go to 9-3 mercifully and very quickly. Farrell pitched their second first half shutout against them (34-0 on September 14) and 38-0 on this night. Another record fell – Kyi's 41st career touchdown pass moved him past Alex Myers in Farrell's record book. Jourdan added to his TD reception record, catching his 51st.

Green and Wright accounted for two touchdowns each. Lewis, Harrison, and Odem each scored once. It was another offensive barrage. But the game was secured by another dominating defensive performance. Total yards: Farrell – 474, West Middlesex – 48. West Middlesex was held to negative twelve yards rushing, and All-State running back Clayton Parish could muster only 32 yards.

Final score 50-6. Next stop, PIAA playoffs.

Jarrett's Game Day Journal – West Middlesex
District 10 Championship

S Nov 10

• Game day. Pre-game. West Middlesex talking trash to our guys
• We are pumped. Fired up
• Great crowd
• Dominate. We fight. We win
• 4 Peat Champs, Baby!
• Momma, I love you!
• 50-6. Team effort. On a mission

The WPIAL – Cradle of Quarterbacks

It is widely known to football fans that high schools of western Pennsylvania have produced a disproportionate number of famous quarterbacks. Chronologically, the QB lineup includes:

Johnny Lujack of Connellsville (Notre Dame)
George Blanda of Youngwood (Kentucky)
Vito (Babe) Parilli of Rochester (Kentucky)
Johnny Unitas of Pittsburgh St. Justin's (Louisville)
Joe Namath of Beaver Falls (Alabama)
Joe Montana of Ringgold (Notre Dame)
Jim Kelly of East Brady (Miami)
Dan Marino of Pittsburgh Central Catholic (Pitt)

If one were to start an automobile tour from the Point in Pittsburgh, he could reach the high school alma maters of each of the eight quarterbacks within an hour. Unitas and Marino were practically neighbors in Pittsburgh, and Parilli and Namath shared hometowns both in the Beaver River Valley. Lujack, Blanda, and Montana all threw their first passes in towns south of Pittsburgh.

These eight quarterbacks were honored with six professional football Hall of Fame inductions:

Unitas 1979
Blanda 1981
Namath 1985
Montana 2000
Kelly 2002
Marino 2005

Lujack won three national championships in his Notre Dame career which culminated in his winning the Heisman Trophy in 1947. Three of them played for the estimable Coach Paul "Bear" Bryant, Parilli and Blanda at Kentucky and Namath at Alabama.

This group of Western PA QB's combined to win ten AFC championships: Parilli (1), Blanda (3), Namath (1), Kelly (4), and Marino (1). Unitas won three NFL championships. The group also earned ten regular season MVP awards, made twelve Super Bowl appearances, and won seven Lombardi Trophies.

They also added to the colorful lore of the story of football. They gave football fans memorable nicknames. "Babe" (Parilli), "Johnny U" (Unitas), "Broadway Joe" (Namath), and "Joe Cool" (Montana).

Blanda made history as he played for the Oakland Raiders until the old football age of 48. Unitas wrote football history as he quarterbacked the Baltimore Colts to the first sudden-death championship game victory. The 1958 NFL championship is known as "The Greatest Game Ever Played." And of course, Namath shocked the football world in Super Bowl III guaranteeing, then quarterbacking, his AFL Jets to a stunning upset of the NFL Colts.

Ironically, the diverse ethnic backgrounds of the group mirrored the historic ethnic diversity of the City of Farrell... Lujack (Polish), Blanda (Slovak), Parilli (Italian), Unitas (Lithuanian), Namath (Hungarian), Montana (Italian), Kelly (Irish), and Marino (Italian/Polish).

The reader might wonder why this side trip to the Cradle of Quarterbacks is included in the story of Farrell football. Well, here is the connection – the Steelers would have to face two more quarterbacks from that Western PA Cradle.

Both Fyfe of Shade High School and Bradley of Our Lady of the Sacred Heart High School far exceeded all eight of the aforementioned legendary Western PA quarterbacks in career and season passing yardage and touchdowns.

It is true that there have been considerable innovations in offensive styles and changes in rules that favor offenses since the Lujack-Blanda-Parilli era. It is also true that the wide-open offenses of the modern era bolster passing statistics. But facts are facts.

In the first round of the PIAA playoffs, Farrell faced the 11-1 Panthers of Shade High School. They were led by Coach Don Fyfe's son, Brady. Fyfe was an All-State QB and a two-time All-State basketball player.

Jarrett's Journal – Shade
PIAA First Round

M Nov 12

- State playoffs. First round vs. Shade
- Thinking we haven't seen a QB or receivers like this
- Coach Huey's report and Omar's game plan are on point

T Nov 13

- Coach Omar assures me they haven't seen a team like us either
- Coach Amp has pneumonia, I'm concerned about his health, but we must grind

W Nov 14

- Amp sends game plan via text
- We thank Neshannock for allowing us to use their field

R Nov 15

- Practices are good
- Bus rides not so good
- Some guys don't know how to act on a bus ride to practice
- Upset that coaches aren't on the bus to supervise shenanigans

F Nov 16

- Game canceled because Somerset won't remove snow
- Don't want their field damaged
- Now I'm upset, routine OFF
- Amp still sick at home – pneumonia – damn
- Find out the game is now Sunday – wow!

S Nov 17

- I'm frustrated, now thinking our team is vulnerable
- We practice at 1:00 pm at Neshannock
- Good practice
- OLSH wins WPIAL – they have a bye into the Western Final

Shade Game Report - PIAA – First Round

The game was originally scheduled to be played at Somerset High School on Saturday, but due to heavy snowfall in the mountains of southwestern PA, the game was moved to another day and another site – Sunday, November 18, Mansion Park—Altoona.

In the previous week Shade had defeated Conemaugh Township for their first ever District 5 championship. They were led by dual threat All-State QB Brady Fyfe, who completed 24 of 28 passes for 270 yards and ran for 94 more in the district championship game.

Against Farrell, Fyfe completed only 7 of 20 passes for 69 yards. One completion went for 48 yards, so the remainder of his throws included 6 completions for 21 yards, 13 incompletions, and 4 interceptions. He was also held to only 27 rushing yards.

After the first quarter the score was 14-8. Then Brian Hilton Jr.'s strip sack which Gary Hopson, Jr. recovered for a touchdown made the score 22-8 which led to an explosion of 34 more unanswered points in the first half.

The coaches agreed to a running clock and eight-minute quarters in the second half. Consequently, the game ended quickly with the score remaining 56-8.

The defense stood tall, as usual, forcing six turnovers and allowing only 92 total yards. Christian had another record-setting performance; his 191 rushing yards raised his season total to 1,922 which surpassed former Ohio State and NFL star Lorenzo Styles' 1,753 yards as Farrell's single season rushing leader.

In addition to the Hopson fumble recovery return, Christian, Jourdan, and Tymir each scored twice and Jaden Harrison once.

In a post-game interview, Kyi told reporter Phillip Cmor of the CHNI News Service, "We've been on a mission since freshman year after losing the state championship game. Every year we've come up one game short. Now we are trying to will our way back there – get over the hump."

To the fans of the Farrell Steelers, it appeared their team was prepared to vault, even soar over that hump. Their record now stood at 12-0. Only eight teams remained in the state. The "hump" was now just three wins in the distance.

Jarrett's Game Day Journal – Shade
PIAA – First Round

S Nov 18

- Team breakfast
- Great focus by players
- Awesome bus ride
- Amp is back – hell yeah!
- Laser focus, defense totally shuts them down
- Crit defensive play of the year
- We score 50 in the first half
- Mercy rule Shade 56-8
- Second half cut short
- Thinking "What a great performance"

Jarrett's Journal – Coudersport
PIAA Quarter Finals

M Nov 19

- Monday game planning
- Waiting to see if Coudersport will win in a rare Monday game

T Nov 20

- Find out we play Coudersport Saturday at Slippery Rock
- My thinking is a little off. I found myself looking at the OLSH Rochester film
- No – no – no don't do it but I was curious

W Nov 21

- Ok, back to Coudersport
- Thinking they got a 2-headed attack. Good QB/good RB who runs tough with heart
- Told team we are going to make history…3 games in 13 days

R Nov 22

- My team embraces this journey
- Chemistry is still excellent
- Laser focus!
- Except a few freshmen

F Nov 23

- Another great walk through
- We ready

Coudersport Game Report – PIAA Quarterfinals

It was the eleventh first half shutout for this version of the "Steel Curtain" defense. On this night on the turf at Slippery Rock University's Milhalik-Thompson Stadium, the Coudersport Falcons did not fly, nor did they run. Farrell's smothering defense allowed only one first down in the first half and allowed only 32 yards for the game.

Kyi continued his accurate passing, going 8 for 8 and three touchdowns following his 6 for 6 and two touchdowns versus Shade. The halftime score was 48-0. It was a familiar storyline… Christian three touchdowns, Jourdan two, and Tymir one. Brian Hilton Jr. continued his excellent kicking, connecting on 6 of 7 PAT's.

Final score was 48-6. Quarterfinals now in the rear-view mirror. The Steelers set their sights on another Western Final for the fourth straight year. This was the "hump" that Kyi referred to that they were unable to surmount in his sophomore and junior
years.

Jarrett's Game Day Journal – Coudersport
PIAA Quarterfinals

S Nov 24

- Slow first quarter
- But then we explode – offense, defense, special teams
- Half ends with Crit's electrifying punt return
- We rout Coudersport 48-6
- After the game, District 9 accused me of running up the score. Wow! Sour grapes
- Tymir injured on big run – bittersweet

Jarrett's Journal – Our Lady of the Sacred Heart
Western Final

M Nov 26

- Coach Huey's game report says – Your team was built for this moment!
- OLSH! OLSH! OLSH!
- Practice at Westminster
- At this point I am obsessed with beating OLSH and the WPIAL
- Did a phone interview with Bob for WPIC Sports on the phone
- Watching practice from the press box

T Nov 27

- Bus ride from Westminster – disaster
- Tymir frustrated because his foot is not healing, goes after a teammate
- I cuss the whole team out
- Told them we will practice at home in Morrison Gym
- I'm upset/nervous

W Nov 28

- Cold and frozen field so we can practice in Morrison Gym
- Believe it or not – good practice
- Confidence coming back
- Great film study
- Vets only need laser focus
- My mental mind game worked
- Got their attention

R Nov 29

- Pre-game practice at Westminster
- We look great!
- Worked on Spartan
- Told Amp it may be time to unleash it
- But depends on the flow of the game
- Thinking to myself – the winner of this game will win the state championship

Our Lady of Sacred Heart Game Report
Western Final

While it is just a 31-mile drive from Farrell High School to Slippery Rock University, the Steelers recognized that the road to Hersheypark is a long one that eluded them the previous two years. Now the only remaining obstacle on their road was the Chargers of OLSH, the WPIAL champions. Just that phrase "WPIAL champs" fueled the fire in Coach Samuels' furnace. Everyone around him had heard him emphatically say, "It's personal for me." The sting of six straight losses to WPIAL teams was at the forefront of his memory and rested unsettled in his soul.

The opponent for this contest was a formidable one. OLSH's record was 12-1, their only loss was to perennial power Jeannette. OLSH averaged 41 points/game. To add to their credentials, they had beaten the other perennial powers, Clairton and Rochester, in the WPIAL playoffs. They were battle-tested and rested due to an unusual playoff bye the previous week. They carried the torch for parochial schools in the current PIAA parochial school vs. public school debate.

If that were not enough to get the Steelers' attention, the Chargers were led by another one of those cats rocked in the cradle of Western PA quarterbacks. Tyler Bradley, son of Coach Dan Bradley, was the second 8,000-yard passer Farrell would face in just three weeks. His season statistics read 3,288 yards and 45 touchdowns, but this would not be Bradley's finest hour.

It is another adage in football that if a potent offense doesn't have the ball, it is not very potent. Defensive coordinator Omar Stewart and Coach Samuels took a page out of Bill Parcell's philosophy of "shortening the game". Meanwhile, offensive coordinator Amp Pegues channeled Knute Rockne and employed his version of the old Notre Dame box formation. Jarrett and Amp called it the "Spartan Package." They had prepared it all season to be unveiled for such a time as this.

It looked like this: 6'3, 240 Kyi at shotgun QB; 5'11, 225 Tymir at FB; 6'4, 282 Kobe at blocking back; and the ever-dangerous

Christian, 6'1, 182 at the other back. All backs aligned on the same side of the backfield. Oh yes, don't forget: you can't load the box and forget split end Jourdan. A formidable formation it was. It was a thing of beauty to watch Kyi let the play clock tick to two seconds, take the snap, and ignite the pulverizing, time-consuming rushing attack.

Farrell spotted OLSH a 23-yard field goal on the first series, only the second time all season they trailed. Then they went to work. The touchdown tally was: Christian three, Kyi two, Jourdan one. Brian converted five of six PATs. Christian reached the 4,000-yard milestone for career rushing yards.

Tymir may have spoken the quote of the season. In describing the physicality of the Spartan package, he claimed, "We knocked the soul out of them!"

Interviewed after the game, a jubilant Coach Samuels with the monkey off his back said, "Stay tuned, we're on our way! We comin', we comin', Farrell High baby, we're comin'." That said it all. Final score was 41-10.

Next stop Hersheypark... PIAA State Championship game.

Jarrett's Game Day Journal – OLSH
Western Final

F Nov 30

- Didn't sleep well!
- But tired of watching films on OLSH
- We ready! Let's go!
- Pre-game speech – my emotions unleashed
- My mom's spirit hits me, talked to the team about how much she loved them
- One year ago, we lost to Jeannette, it was the last game she saw me coach and them play
- Good omens and vibes this week
- Quiet confidence inside me
- I hear my mom's voice during the National Anthem – "Victory is yours tonight son" – Faith
- In pre-game, I hear Kyi yell, "Yeah, we're the best team in the state!"
- To me that was the turning point of the game
- First drive when they only got a field goal… I knew then we would shut down their high-powered offense
- Great strategy – Spartan formation unleashed
- First TD, JT hops, jumps, dives into the end zone
- We hit them with body blows, ran right at them and around them
- Crit was great
- Kyi was amazing
- Defense great
- Finally beat WPIAL – OLSH
- Tears of joy
- 41-10

Jarrett's Journal – Lackawanna Trail
State Championship Game

M Dec 3

- On to the State Championship Our send-off was amazing
- Very confident as we prepare for Lackawanna Trail
- It wasn't a cockiness, but we knew our biggest mental and physical challenge was the OLSH game
- But it's time to move on

T Dec 4

- After 3 days of practice prep, Sunday, Monday, Tuesday with our green military minded – "Once a Steeler always a Steeler" hoodies on
- Our send-off was amazing
- Missing mom still
- But confident
- Upset we couldn't stay an extra night to support Wilmington

W Dec 5

- Practice at the Milton Hershey School was good
- JT tweaked ankle
- Tymir feeling better
- Omar throws team out of film study, once again too jovial
- Me – I'm laughing! I know by now we are ready

Chapter 6

The Best Seat in the House

"...a scintillating 20-yard run...wiggle to the left, skip to the right, jump-cut, stiff arm...(Christian Lewis)

"...a memorable rumbling, high-stepping, tackle-breaking 56-yard touchdown..." (Kyi Wright)

Chapter 6

The Best Seat in the House

There is a spectacle in sports that rarely gets reported. It is that moment when you first see your team as they enter the arena, resplendent in the uniforms that represent your school.

This was a moment such as that. The Farrell Steelers football team gathered as they always did. They were outfitted in the fashionable "uniforms" favored by young men of 2018. The "lineup" on this day best defined the character of this team.

This day was March 3, 2018. This was not a ball game but rather a moment of greater significance. The site was the Greater New and Living Way Temple of the Apostolic Church in Sharon, PA.

The occasion was the funeral service of Kathy Stewart, who had passed away on February 24. She was the president of the Farrell Football Boosters, the best friend and biggest fan of Coach Jarrett Samuels, and his beloved mother.

In 2011, Jarrett had taken a sabbatical leave from coaching for a year to care for Kathy after her cancer diagnosis. Kathy's remission allowed her to cheer for her son and the Steelers for six more years. Then at the time of the Western Final in 2017, her cancer recurred. Three months later she would enter her heavenly home.

Coach Samuels approached the 2018 season with a broken heart, but with the assurance and memories of his mother's love. And he knew she was still rooting for him as she always had.

The chords of Steven Wariner's song 'Holes in the Floor of Heaven' rang true in Coach Samuels' heart. "There's 'holes in the floor of heaven'…And her tears are pourin' down…She's watchin' over me."

Kathy took her rightful place in "The Best Seat in the House' watching over her son 'through those holes in the floor of heaven' as he coached the most important game. Coach Samuels and the team had dedicated the season to her. It was appropriate that she had the Best Seat in the House.

The day was Thursday, December 6, 2018, the hour was 1:00. The site was Hersheypark Stadium. The occasion was the PIAA state championship. The contestants: Farrell High School Steelers (14-0) out of District 10 versus the Lions of Lackawanna Trail High School (14-1) out of District 2.

The Farrell Steelers emerged from the locker room now clad in their other uniforms… the classy uniforms fit for battle… navy blue pants, jerseys, and helmets with gold numerals.

Coach Samuels approached the game with the belief that their best game was still within them.

The weatherman greeted the Steelers with sunny skies and 44 degrees but a quartering wind out of the southeast rendered a much chillier feel.

This was the culminating moment in the 100th year of Farrell High School Football.

In this season in which almost everything went right… in the first minute of the championship game, everything went wrong.

The play-by-play of the first 37 seconds read like this:

• Farrell assessed an illegal procedure penalty before the opening kickoff
• Jourdan fumbled the kickoff, Lackawanna recovered on the 26-yard line
• Before the first play from scrimmage, Farrell penalized for an illegal substitution
• Lackawanna first play, a screen pass, went to the 11-yard line
• Their second play, a sweep, resulted in a touchdown

All of that in just 37 seconds. **Lackawanna Trail – 7 Farrell – 0**

As you know by now, the Steelers almost never trailed. Well, it only lasted for 45 seconds. Here is the play-by-play of Farrell's first possession:

• Jourdan returned the kickoff 38 yards to the 45-yard line
• Christian accelerated and hurdled on a toss sweep to the left for 16
• Christian took a handoff from Kyi on a traditional I formation lead play.

He executed his signature spin move in the hole, then cut to the right, switched the ball to his outside arm, and eased into the end zone from 40 yards out. In his typical touchdown "celebration," he set the ball down in the endzone and ran to his sideline.

That was a 55-yard "drive" in two plays and Christian's 34th touchdown of the season. There would be four more to come today. His 55 rushing yards were the first of what would be 249 by days end. A Brian Hilton, Jr. PAT out of Christian Hartley's hold tied the **score at 7-7** just 1:08 into the game.

The Lions then mounted their most sustained drive of the game, 12 plays – 51 yards which ended in a shanked field goal attempt. Unfortunately, LT's botched field goal went out of bounds at the two-yard line, where by rule, the Steelers took possession.

A 98-yard, 6 play, 2:24 drive ensued. The drive featured a 54-yard pass from Kyi to Hilton, Jr. who was split right and uncovered. The ever-savvy Kyi noted the defensive misalignment, tapped his helmet to signal to Brian, then delivered the pass which put the ball on the 34-yard line.

Christian finished the drive with a scintillating 20-yard run...wiggle to the left, skip to the right, jump-cut, stiff arm...then, as usual, just set the ball down in the end zone. His touchdown total was now at two.

Farrell – 14 Lackawanna – 7. That is how the first quarter ended.

Part way through the quarter, in a classy act of neighborly sportsmanship, Wilmington Coach Brandon Phillian led his Greyhound team into the grandstands to cheer for their district rivals. Wilmington was in Hershey early to prepare for their championship game on Friday. Recognizing their entry, in a similar act of sportsmanship, the Farrell fans rose as one to acknowledge the Greyhounds. It was a good District 10 moment.

The next LT possession consisted of six plays and totaled 16 yards.

The next Farrell drive – 4 plays, 75 yards. Christian took a pitch to the left side, broke two tackles and showed his sprinter speed, 53 yards for a touchdown. That's three.

Farrell – 21 - Lackawanna – 7

Next LT drive mustered only one yard and ended with a Hilton, Jr. strip and a diving Juwon Samuels fumble recovery.

Farrell took possession at the LT 37-yard line. Three plays later Jourdan swept right, a spectacular diving effort landed him in the end zone. (The Steelers benefitted from the absence of video replay as his knee was down on the three-yard line). His effort was rewarded but he was injured on the play. One of the compelling images of the game was Kyi and Christian carrying their teammate and friend all the way across the field to the sideline. The extra point was blocked.

Farrell – 27 Lackawanna – 7

Next LT drive, four plays and 25 yards ended with Dashon Sims tipping a pass that was intercepted by Tymir Green.

Farrell's next "drive" was just one play. It was a memorable rumbling, high-stepping, tackle-breaking, 56-yard touchdown run by Kyi on a designed quarterback keep.

Farrell - 34 - Lackawanna – 7

Next LT drive, four plays and zero yards ended with a Tyree Hammonds interception.

Farrell continued their pulverizing ground attack on the last drive of the half. Seven plays, 60 yards, 2:16, ended with Kyi bouncing to the outside and stretching to the pylon for the sixth touchdown of the first half…38 seconds remained.

Christian took a direct snap and converted the two-point try. That made the **score 42-7** which enacted the mercy rule (35-point lead) for the entire second half. While the decision to go for two may have been questioned by some as unsportsmanlike, Coach Samuels was just taking advantage of the rules of the game. It was the proper coaching decision.

First Half Summary

Scoring drives:
2 plays, 55 yards, :31
6 plays, 98 yards, 2:24
4 plays, 75 yards, 1:31
3 plays, 37 yards, :45
1 play, 56 yards, :12
7 plays, 60 yards, 2:12

Farrell 16.5 yards/play
LT 3.2 yards/play

With the mercy clock running, the second half moved along quickly. Farrell possessed the ball for 10 plays and LT held it for only eight in the third quarter. The scoreboard registered another Christian touchdown in the third quarter (5 plays, 40 yards, 12-yard TD) **(score 48-7)** and then again on the first play of the fourth quarter (6 plays, 70 yards, 28-yard TD), on a swerving run on a draw play **(55-7)**.

Dashon Sims who had pleaded to run down with the kickoff team got his wish after the last touchdown. His spectacular hit on the ballcarrier was penalized as illegal. Replay indicated that it was not. But you can't fault the officials because they may have never seen such a hit. Legal or illegal, it put an exclamation point on this resounding victory.

The Lions scored two meaningless touchdowns on a pair of eight play drives as the clock wound down.

Final Score...Steelers - 55 - Lackawanna – 20

Endearing images from the game were the well-designed curtain call for the seniors with 6:17 remaining which was greeted by a warm standing ovation from the chilly Farrell faithful. Coach Samuels then greeted Heart and Soul:

#75 (Hobson, Jr.), #54 (Satterwhite III), #50 (Purdie), # 66 (Hopson, Jr.), #57 (Hilton), #58 (Sims)

One at a time as they came off the field for the last time. It was his acknowledgement that games are still won at the line of scrimmage. In the post-game interview, Coach Samuels, "Upfront our guys did the job. I told you back in the summer, we weren't going to the state championship unless our guys up front did the job. 'Heart and Soul' did the job for us. I'm so proud of them."

Upon further reflection about this team with the Herald's Ed Farrell, Samuels again, "You won't find another group like this. You can have an adult conversation with the guys on this team, something you can't have with many kids these days. That goes back to their upbringing and a lot of credit goes to their parents. I thank God for their parents and for allowing me to coach 'em. We do coach 'em hard but we do love 'em."

Further in post-game interviews:

"This is a brotherhood. After comin' here freshman year and losing to be able to make it back and win...it is just a blessing," said Christian Lewis after his five-touchdown performance.

Coach Samuels last statement was the memory of his mom and the reminder to everyone that the season, and now the championship was dedicated to her.

"If you wrote a book about it, it couldn't have been scripted better," Coach Samuels.

Well, you just read the book.

The lady who occupied the "Best Seat in the House," didn't have to read it because she saw it all through the 'Holes in the Floor of Heaven'.

Jarrett's Game Day Journal – Lackawanna Trail

State Championship Game

R. Dec 6

- Game Day
- Good team breakfast
- Good vibes. Slept good
- Reflected on the process/journey and of course, Momma
- Entering the stadium for pre-game, suddenly the skies opened up and the sun glared through brightly
- I say to myself, my Momma is here!
- I knew she would not miss the big one!
- Pre-game speech was good
- Guys were loose, break dancing on the field before the game
- National anthem – Wow!
- First play – penalty offsides
- Second play – kickoff return – JT fumbles
- Two plays later they score…Me – I'm calm/stoic. Thinking "OK, we are good"
- Hearing Mom's voice say, "Baby boy, I didn't bring you this far to let you fail"
- O line, Crit, Defense, Kyi
- And we start the avalanche
- 55 unanswered points
- State game over by halftime
- I never wished the clock to unwind faster that I did in the second half
- Coaches and team composed ourselves before the half after an altercation
- We came out with class in the second half
- Fourth Quarter – the reality of our accomplishment began to settle in. Tears of joy pouring the entire quarter. Celebration begins. What a year! 100 years of football! What a season! What a team! The best ever! 15 – 0! Undefeated!

- Undisputed champs. I kissed the trophy. Kathy's team did it. Kathy's blessing did it. This senior class, this team, dedicated this season to her. Her baby boy.
- Thinking if I wrote a book, the script ended to perfection. What a great book this would be. A best seller. What a movie script. Thinking about all my emotions. All my past team's failures. My emotions are everywhere.
- Thinking no matter what happens in my life. I will always be, we will always be state champions. 30 years I chased this trophy. Now forever it's mine. Proud of my staff, my team, my city of Farrell...and all of our supporters. My brother and sister were there. Everyone I love was there. Kathy's blessings!

M Dec 17

- On cloud 20!
- Enjoying the title "State Champions"
- We did it
- Quadruple crown winners
- All goals achieved
- Now assisting the seniors in college signings/preparations
- Love my team...organization, booster club, parents, school district
- City of Champs once again!
- Christmas came early
- Blessed team

Chapter 7

Farrell Football

"...this was a fast, skilled, tough, smart team that maximized
its God-given talents..."

"...in this city made famous by men tasked with
making steel, the coaches understood that their task
was to mold the steel in the men."

Chapter 7

Farrell Football

District 10

November 2... Reynolds 62-6 @ Hickory High School
*November 10...West Middlesex 50-6 @ Wilmington Area High School

PIAA

November 18... Shade 56-8 @ Mansion Park Altoona
November 24...48-6 Coudersport @ Slippery Rock University
**November 26...Our Lady of the Sacred Heart 41-10 @ Slippery Rock University
***December 6...Lackawanna Trail 55-20 @ Hersheypark Stadium

*District 10 Championship
**Western Final
***State Championship

Shade – PIAA First Round

Farrell		Shade
23	First Downs	5
376	Rushing Yards	23
108	Passing Yards	69
6-6-0	Att-Comp-Int	20-7-4
484	Total Yards	92
3-1	Fumbles/Lost	2-2
9-84	Penalties/Yards	6-45
Farrell	22 – 34 – 0 – 0 … 56	
Shade	8 – 0 – 0 – 0 … 0	

Coudersport – PIAA Quarterfinals

Farrell		Coudersport
20	First Downs	4
313	Rushing Yards	117
187	Passing Yards	11
12-11-0	Att-Comp-Int	1-4-0
500	Total Yards	128
3-2	Fumbles/Lost	4-2
6-35	Penalties/Yards	3-11
Farrell	14 – 34 – 0 – 0 …48	
Coudersport	0 – 0 – 6 – 0 …6	

Our Lady of the Sacred Heart – Western Final

Farrell		OLSH
16	First Downs	11
336	Rushing Yards	52
14	Passing Yards	108
4-2-1	Att-Comp-Int	22-10-1
350	Total Yards	160
0-0	Fumbles/Lost	3-0
10-77	Penalties/Yards	5-44
Farrell	7 – 21 – 7 – 6 … 41	
OLSH	3 – 0 – 7 – 0 … 10	

Lockawanna Trail – PIAA State Championship

Farrell		Lackawanna Trail
20	First Downs	14
389	Rushing Yards	154
111	Passing Yards	40
4-4-0	Att-Comp-Int	12-6-2
500	Total Yards	194
2-2	Fumbles/Lost	2-1
7-76	Penalties/Yards	2-10
Farrell	14 – 28 – 6 – 7 … 55	
Lackawanna Trail	7 – 0 – 0 – 13 … 20	

Team Roster
2018 Farrell High School Steelers

Number & Name	Position	Year	Size
1 – Christian Lewis	RB, CB	Sr	6-1, 182
2 – Kyi Wright	QB, LB	Sr	6-3, 240
3 – Elijah Harper	WR, S	Sr	5-8, 157
5 – Jourdan Townsend	WR, S	Sr	6-0, 184
7 – Natoreus Atwood	RB, OLB	Sr	6-0, 190
8 – Everton Rawlins	WR, CB	Sr	6-0, 165
9 – Jaden Harrison	RB, CB	So	5-9, 158
10 – Christian Hartley	QB, OLB	So	5-9, 170
11 – Omar Stewart, Jr.	WR, CB	Fr	6-1, 157
12 – Brian Hilton, Jr.	WR, DE	Jr	6-2, 182
13 – Brice Butler	RB, S	So	5-7, 155
14 – Trian Holden	QB, S	Fr	5-8, 155
15 – Amarion Odem	WR, CB	So	6-1, 170
17 – Ray Raver	QB, S	Jr	5-10, 160
20 – Tyree Hammonds	RB, OLB	Jr	5-8, 155
22 – Tymir Green	FB, MLB	Sr	5-11, 225
23 – Anthony Jackson	RB, OLB	Fr	5-9, 175
24 – Juwon Samuels	WR, CB	Jr	5-9, 170
25 – Cameron Zimmerman	RB, OLB	Sr	5-11, 185
26 – Sayvion Thomas	RB, DE	Jr	5-10, 165
27 – Taidon Strickland	FB, LB	Fr	5-8, 160
31 – Jalen Russell	RB, LB	Jr	5-7, 160
32 – Anthony Stallworth	RB, OLB	Fr	5-10, 163
33 – Adrian Daniels	RB, DE	Jr	6-4, 240
44 – Dwight Ravenscraft	RB, LB	Jr	5-9, 260
50 – Vincent Purdie	OL, DL	Sr	5-9, 260
51 – Robert Spence	OL, DL	Jr	6-1, 214
52 – Jaden Howell	OL, DL	Fr	5-7, 165
53 – Ronald Lacamera, Jr.	OL, DL	Jr	5-9, 302
54 – Gary Satterwhite III	OL, DL	So	6-3, 282
55 – Jaiman Holden	OL, DL	Fr	6-1, 244
56 – Preston Williams	OL, DL	Fr	6-0, 325
57 – Kobe Hilton	OL, DL	Sr	6-4, 283
58 – Dashon Sims	OL, DL	Sr	6-2, 278
66 – Gary Hopson, Jr.	OL, DL	Jr	6-0, 310
75 – Melvin Hobson, Jr.	OL, DL	Jr	6-3, 290

Post Season Honors
District 10 All Region
Erie Times-News

First Team Offense
Kyi Wright QB
Christian Lewis RB
Tymir Green AP
Jourdan Townsend WR
Brian Hilton, Jr. WR
Kobe Hilton OL
Dashon Sims OL
Gary Satterwhite III OL

Second Team Offense
Gary Hopson, Jr. OL
Melvin Hobson, Jr. OL

First Team Defense
Kobe Hilton DL
Gary Hopson DL
Brian Hilton, Jr. DL
Kyi Wright LB
Tymir Green LB
Tyrie Hammonds LB
Jourdan Townsend DB
Elijah Harper DB

Second Team Defense
Juwon Samuels DB

Region Player of the Year
Christian Lewis

Pennsylvania Football Writers
All-State First Team

Kyi Wright QB
Christian Lewis RB
Jourdan Townsend WR
Kobe Hilton OL
Gary Satterwhite III OL
Tymir Green LB

Player of the Year – Kyi Wright
Coach of the Year – Jarrett Samuels

PAFootballNews.com
First Team Offense

Christian Lewis RB
Jourdan Townsend WR
Kobe Hilton OT
Gary Satterwhite III C

First Team Defense

Gary Hopson, Jr. DT
Brian Hilton, Jr. DE
Tymir Green OLB
Kyi Wright MLB
Juwon Samuels DB

USA Today's All USA-PA

Second Team

Kobe Hilton OL
Kyi Wright LB

Erie Times News
Varsity Cup All Stars

First Team Offense

Melvin Hobson, Jr.
Christian Lewis
Jourdan Townsend

First Team Defense

Tymir Green
Kobe Hilton
Kyi Wright

Small School Player of the Year

Christian Lewis

Male Athlete of the Year

Kyi Wright

Coach of the Year

Jarrett Samuels

Team of the Year

Farrell Steelers Football

Coaching Staff

There are many coaches who are blessed with talented players. But fewer is the number of coaches who utilize that talent to the utmost.

Coach Samuels effectively guided his dedicated and knowledgeable staff toward the goal of maximizing the potential of their gifted players. Just as an athlete is measured by his capability to seek the most from his ability, so too, the same can be said of coaches.

Even a novice fan could recognize the speed and skill of this team. What may have been missed by the casual observer was the physicality and intelligence of the group. They were a selfless team that exhibited a joy in their teammates' successes and a bolstering of each other when necessary. Both the coaches and players recognized that hard work combined with meticulous preparation would give them the best opportunity to dictate the outcome.

The coaches' extensive film study and detailed preparation matched that of college coaches. The staff mentored, taught, encouraged, and challenged the team toward their ultimate goal.

It could truly be said that this was a fast, skilled, tough, smart team that maximized its God-given talents… and a team that was very well prepared and very well coached.

It has been said that in this city made famous by men tasked with making steel, the coaches understood their task was to mold the steel in the men.

The Farrell Steeler bloodlines run deep. The entire staff once wore the Farrell blue and gold jerseys. Many went on to successful college playing careers. Among them, Samuels at Westminster, Pegues at Grambling and Slippery Rock, Stewart at IUP, Newell at Grambling, Trudo at Syracuse, Falconi at Edinboro.

Amp and Bucky were key players on Coach Falconi's back-to-back state championships in 1995 and 1996. Amp was under center at quarterback in 1995 and Bucky led a stalwart defense.

Jarrett Samuels' Westminster Titan teams compiled a 38-9 record with four national playoff appearances during his four-year linebacking career. Bucky Newell won the first ever prestigious Eddie Robinson Award at Grambling. Robert Trudo was a team captain at Syracuse and an All-Academic honoree.

The staff's family ties ran even deeper. Jarrett had to wait seven months for his uncle, and later to be Defensive Coordinator, Omar Stewart, to be born. Omar Stewart, Jr. played wide receiver/linebacker on this team. Jarrett's son, Juwon (JuJu), was an All-State defensive back. And Kyi Wright is Jarrett's nephew.

Bucky Newell's son Malachi was the Pennsylvania State Defensive Player of the Year in 2015. Coach Troy Harrison (Jaden), Robbie Townsend (Jourdan), and Brian Hilton, Sr. (Kobe and Brian Hilton, Jr.) all had sons who played important roles on this team.

The Coaching Staff

Jarrett Samuels – Head Coach
Anthony "Amp" Pegues – Offensive Coordinator
Omar Stewart – Defensive Coordinator
Dante "Bucky" Newell – Defensive Line
Victor Phillips – Offensive Line
Troy Harrison – Running Backs
Lamont Samuels – Defensive Backs/Special Teams
Robert Trudo – Offensive Line
Robbie Townsend – Offensive Line
Emil Debonis – Strength/Conditioning
Brian Hilton, Sr. – Middle School
Kurt Chester – Middle School
Jason Marshall – Middle School
Darwin Dixon – Statistics
Warren Robinson – Kickers
Sam Phillips – Middle School
Lou Falconi – Senior Consultant

Support Staff

Dan Dragicevic – Athletic Director
Jim Cardamon – Assistant Athletic Director
Dan Braatz – Trainer
Robert Multari – Team Doctor
Pat Chovan – Uniforms
Colleen De'Angelo – Video
Tracey Samuels – Booster Club
Lora Adams-King – Superintendent
Matt Fowler – Principal
Brian Vecchia – Assistant Principal

Farrell Football Family

Family ties run deeply in the Farrell sports family. For example, here are a few:

2 – Kyi Wright – Mother, Kavon Wright, All-State volleyball champion
5 – Jourdan Townsend – Father, Coach Robbie Townsend
9 – Jaden Harrison – Father, Coach Troy Harrison
11 – Omar Stewart, Jr. – Father, Coach Omar Stewart
12 – Brian Hilton, Jr. – Father, Coach Brian Hilton, Sr.
20 – Tyree Hammonds – Mother, Tiffany Hodges, All-State volleyball champion
22 – Tymir Green – Mother, Maggie Green, All-State volleyball champion
24 – Juwon Samuels – Father, Coach Jarrett Samuels, uncle, Coach Omar Stewart
33 – Adrian Daniels – Brother, Carlos Daniels, football champion '95, '96
54 – Gary Satterwhite III – Father, three-time basketball state champion at Kennedy Christian
57 – Kobe Hilton – Father, Brian, Sr., brother Brian, Jr.
75 – Melvin Hobson – Grandfather, Dan Scarvel, assistant coach with Lou Falconi
Lamont Samuels, Jr. – manager, son of Lamont Samuels
Aaron Pegues – manager, son of Amp Pegues

Chapter Eight

Sports Fantasies

- Jesse – Berlin Olympic Stadium,1936

- Jackie – Ebbets Field, 1947

- Willie – Rickwood Field, 1947

- Texas Western, Cole Fieldhouse, 1966

Farrell Sports Fantasies

- Big Dog

- A Man Named Julius

- Maurice…The Integration of College Basketball

- Wilt… December 28, 1954

- Old Section 3

- Bob and Jennifer…1986, 1987, 1988

- Back-to-Back…1995, 1996

A Sports Fan's Fantasy

If a sports fan could travel back in time, where would he go and what would he want to see? This author has often mused about this enticing hypothetical.

Jesse

My journey begins in August of 1936 in Berlin, Nazi
Germany. I arrive with some political trepidation, a good bit of Olympic
excitement, and American pride. I squeeze among 100,000 spectators for
the track and field events. My seat is directly in front of the
Führer's private box. I then cheer proudly, smugly, and enthusiastically
as Jesse Owens mounts the podium to receive one, two, three, four gold
medals to the dismay and disgust of the Führer. I can't help but peek up
at the Führer's box...he's gone.

You can read Jesse's Olympic story and the inspiring act of
sportsmanship by his German competitor, Luz Long, in Jeremy
Schapp's book, *Triumph, the Untold Story of Jesse Owens and Hitler's
Olympics.*

Jackie

My second stop is Brooklyn, New York – Jackie at Ebbets Field.
It is April of 1947. I delight in watching my favorite player flouncing
down the third baseline, his loose-fitting jersey number 42 flouncing
with him. His exaggerated movements taunt and dare the pitcher as he
comes into the stretch position on the mound. And then in an instant his
spikes create a flurry of dust as Jackie Robinson dashes to steal home.

There is a broad collection of Jackie Robinson books, one of the
best is Arnold Rampersad's, *Jackie Robinson: A Biography.*

Willie

My third visit is to the historic Rickwood Field in Birmingham,
Alabama. It is still 1947. A sixteen-year-old kid playing with grown men
quickly grabs my attention. His sleek body gracefully glides across the

greensward which is centerfield. His cap flies off, his glove and his hand form a basket at waist level and the long fly ball nestles in his glove. The graceful glide, the flying cap, and the basket catch would become the signatures of the Sey Hey Kid – Willie Mays.

A deep look into the life of Willie can be found in two good books, Allen Barra's, *Rickwood Field: A Century in America's Oldest Ballpark* and *Willie Mays: The Life, The Legend* by James S. Hirsch.

Texas Western

My last visit on this fantastic journey takes me to Cole Fieldhouse, College Park, Maryland. It is March 19, 1966. I cheer for the unknown underdogs from an unknown school, with unknown players. It is the NCAA basketball championship game. I cheer for the Texas Western Miners and guys named Big Daddy, Nevil, Bobby Joe, Orsten and Willie Cager. They upset the known, vaunted, blue-blood, all-White Kentucky Wildcats of Coach Adolph Rupp. Five Black players defeat five White players. That was the first time ever. That was history rivaling Jackie's breaking of baseball's color barrier nineteen years earlier.

Well, that's my journey. Where does yours take you?

Farrell Sports Fantasies

Now here's my journey through the storied history of the Steelers of Farrell High School.

Big Dog

The first stop on my journey explores the mysterious story of Henry Thomas. Henry is not as well-known as the more recent Farrell elite athletes. The year is 1938. I would love to have interviewed Mr. Thomas.

Henry grew up on Hamilton Avenue in Farrell. He also grew up to be known as 'Big Dog'.

Henry was a formidable force in both football and basketball. In the spectacular history of Farrell basketball, Henry was the first Steeler named All-State in 1938. Perhaps the first Black player so honored in the Commonwealth.

In the fall of 1938, the Steelers compiled their best record (8-1) in the 21-year history of the football program. But the official record book indicates a record of 0-9-0. You see, despite the Big Dog's sensational play at the left end, it was discovered that he was ineligible because of his age. So, the county and district championship as well as the victories were expunged from the record book. The same fate would be received by the 1939 basketball team.

The saga of Henry Thomas then continued at the HBCU, Lincoln University in Jefferson City, Missouri where he again excelled on the football field and the basketball court. Then he disappeared only to re-appear two years later at another HBCU, North Carolina College (now North Carolina Central). Again, Henry played a significant role as a receiver on the conference championship team. And yet again, the season was forfeited because Henry was declared ineligible due to a transfer rule violation.

The fall of next year, 1942, the destination for the peripatetic Thomas was the integrated University of Toledo Rockets basketball team. But his time there was short-lived as Uncle Sam and the United States Navy had other plans for him. His military service was short-lived, also, as he was deemed attitudinally unfit just a short time later.

Then in the fall of 1943 he re-appeared at North Carolina College to play basketball for the legendary John McClendon, the pioneering Black coach who revolutionized the game with a full court pressing, fast-paced style.

In the spring of 1944, he disappeared from campus only to re-appear on the semi-professional circuit in New Jersey and New York City. It is rumored that he may have played on occasions for Farrell's famous Twin City Elks.

His is the colorful story of extraordinary talent, controversial decisions, sociological challenges, and intriguing mystery... of appearances and disappearances... of championships and forfeits.

You can read more about Henry in Scoot Ellsworth brilliant book, *The Secret Game (A Wartime Story of Courage, Change, and Basketball's Lost Triumph)*.

A Man Named Julius

My most anticipated stop on this Farrell Sports Fantasy tour is approached with a deep sense of respectful awe.

I see a skinny kid dribbling a well-worn basketball on the hard packed dirt playground at the old J.A. Farrell School at the corner of Spearman and Staunton. I watch as he lofts shot after left-handed shot at the bent hoop with no net. He looks to be about nine years old.

He seems different from other young boys, as this solitary activity is pursued with an uncommon earnestness. The world is rumbling with war in Europe and the scent of war is approaching America's shore... but on this day this young boy's focus is only on that hoop.

Not being a native of this area, I was not familiar with the important names in Farrell. It didn't take long to learn that there was one name that stood above all others.

I now realize that the solitary figure on the playground was the young Julius McCoy who had recently moved to Farrell from Cheraw, SC, just as so many Farrell residents had.

Julius would grow up to lead Farrell to their first state championship in basketball in 1952 and to their first football WPIAL championship in 1951.

After graduation from Farrell High School, Julius matriculated at Michigan State University. There he averaged 20.9 points per game for the Spartans. In 1956 he earned third team All-American recognition, first team All-Big Ten honors, and the MSU Athlete of the Year award.

He was drafted by the St. Louis Hawks but it was not an opportune time in history for a Black man in that league in that city. Julius then went on to a long career as one of the greats in the Eastern Basketball Association.

Jim Raykie, the highly respected former editor of the *Sharon Herald*, was born the year Julius led the Steelers to their first state championship. He grew up in Farrell idolizing Julius. He wrote with reverent respect about the transcendent influence and the mystique of Julius McCoy.

Gary Swanson, the voice of the famous Gus Macker Tournament was a young man when he met Julius. Although Julius was an imposing man, Gary was struck by the warmth of his smile, his inviting gracious manner, and the class with which he carried himself.

You will not find an ill word spoken about Julius.

Here is a sampling of tributes to Julius:

*"His character, work ethic, quiet leadership... he was
bigger than life – that I tried to model."*
Col. Don Jones (ret)
1956 state championship team
Teammate of Jimmy McCoy

*"Above all, Julius was always a gentleman, always a family man
... well respected. He's a legend in Farrell."*
Dr. Jim Kollar
1954 state championship team

*"He was the guy we all looked up to... we all wanted to be like
Julius McCoy. He set the standard for all of us. He was a superstar."*
Dr. Brian Generalovich
1959, 1960 state championship teams
All-State football and basketball
University of Pittsburgh star

*"A great man, a true gentleman... inspirational leader. He will
always be the Steelers Most Valuable Player."*
Jack Marin (1962)
All-State
All-American at Duke
NBA All Star

Oh, how I wish I could have met Julius McCoy! I was drawn to
him by not only his athletic excellence, but also by the transcendence of
his personality and his influence.

By all accounts, he was a highly respected gentleman who carried himself with a quiet dignity, who in this small town will forever be held in the highest esteem.

When I started this project, I asked my college roommate and former Westminster Titan, Tom Ritchey, about Farrell. He said, "Everybody talks about Julius." That inspired this stop on my Farrell Sports Fantasy tour.

While nobody knew about the mysterious story of Henry Thomas, everybody still talks about Julius.

Maurice

The story of Maurice Stokes is both tragic and inspiring. Stokes was a star basketball player at Westinghouse High School.

Ironically, his last high school game was a loss to Farrell in 1951. With four seconds remaining in the game, a left-handed hook by Farrell's Julius "Hooks" McCoy sealed the 55-54 victory. That game propelled Farrell to the state championship game which they lost to Coatesville 66-55.

The next year, Julius' senior year, the Steelers won their first state championship. After graduation from Westinghouse, Maurice enrolled at St. Francis (PA) College with his Westinghouse High School teammate Eugene Phelps.

Integration of College Basketball

My Farrell sports fantasy tour takes me to tiny Loretto, PA, the home of St. Francis. In the 1950's, college basketball was largely not yet integrated. Farrell played a significant role in this important social change.

Most Black athletes played at HBCU's in the South. It was rare for a northern team to have more than one or two Black players. Stokes and Phelps were joined by Farrell's Marion Lampkins and Bobby Jones, giving the Red Flash four Black players in 1952.

Much attention has been given to the 1955 University of San Francisco team with Bill Russell, KC Jones and Hal Perry that defeated La Salle 77-63 to win the national championship.

Next, Loyola of Chicago started the 1963 national championship, a 60-58 win over Cincinnati, with Jerry Harkness, Vic Rouse, Les Hunter, and Ron Miller. Four Black players.

The most famous game, of course, was the 1966 Texas Western Miners vs. Kentucky for the national championship. The first time ever with an all-Black starting lineup:

Big Daddy David Lattin
Bobby Joe Hill
Orsten Artis
Willie Cager
Willie Worsley...

upset the all-White Wildcats 72-65.

The reason for this stop on the fantasy tour was to identify Farrell's significant contribution to the integration of college basketball.

The story started with the great Maurice Stokes whose professional basketball career ended in 1958 when a head injury suffered in a game left him paralyzed. That's the tragic part.

The inspiring part is that his Cincinnati Royals teammate, Jack Twyman, ironically also originally from Pittsburgh (Central Catholic), assumed the demanding compassionate role of caretaker for the rest of Maurice's life.

You can read about this story of a White man's selfless care for his Black teammate...the moving story of an ultimate teammate. The book is Pat Farabaugh's... *An Unbreakable Bond.*

Read about the historic Texas Western game in Frank Fitzpatrick's book, *Walls Came Tumbling Down.*

Wilt
December 28, 1954

My Farrell Sports fantasy transports me to the annual Lions Club Tournament on December 28, 1954. It was the most anticipated event in the illustrious history of Farrell High School sports. This was the day that Wilt Chamberlain would come to town.

My friend, Janet Chisholm Shannon, who was Coach McCluskey's student assistant gave me a first-hand account of the excitement in the build-up to the game, and the frantic pursuit of tickets. She knew the story well because she was selling the tickets.

Wilt's Philadelphia Overbook teams won the highly competitive Philadelphia City League in his junior year (20-0) and his senior year (18-1).

Wilt averaged 47.2 points per game as a senior. He even scored 90 in one game that season. But his 33 points on this night would not be enough as the Steelers maintained their 73-game home winning streak. The final score: Overbrook – 58, Farrell – 59.

Overbrook would conclude their season by defeating West Philadelphia for the City League championship at the historic house of hoops, the Palestra on the University of Pennsylvania campus.

That proved that Wilt could win at the Palestra but not at the gym that would, in later years, be named in honor of Coach McCluskey.

Overbrook – 58

	G	F	Pts
Sadler	9	2-4	9
Hughes	3	1-1	7
Chamberlain	12	9-15	33
Miller	2	0-0	4
Leaman	3	0-2	2
Johnson	1	0-2	2

Farrell – 59

	G	F	Pts
Kemp	6	3-5	15
McCoy	7	5-9	19
Bayer	2	0-1	4
Hall	0	1-3	1
Gustas	0	8-10	8
Jones	5	2-4	12

You, too, can take this fantasy trip. There is a recently discovered grainy home movie of it on the internet. The presence of Wilt is unmistakable. As you observe the massive crowd crammed into the gym… you can feel the tension, the excitement, the joy of this amazing event.

There are many books about Wilt, among them Robert Cherry's, *Wilt: Larger than Life.*

Old Section 3

My fantastic journey takes me to a sports bar. I settle in a booth amongst a bunch of old jocks who regale me with tales of old Section 3.

Times have changed, school enrollments have shifted, demography has been altered, and economic health has waned but many still glory in the "Old Section 3 Days". Tales still abound about exploits and upsets, about amazing victories and stunning defeats, and about the greats who competed in Section 3 and those who got greater as the years progressed. Some of the tales are even true … most of them are colorful.

Old Section 3
- **Farrell**
- **Sharon**
- **Butler**
- **Ellwood City**
- **New Castle**
- **Aliquippa**
- **Ambridge**
- **Beaver Falls**

The Farrell Steelers surely added their share of greatness to this legacy, particularly in football and basketball.

The names of opponents flow easily in tavern conversations among those who remember the 50's and 60's… Namath of Beaver

Falls, Hanratty of Butler, Ditka of Aliquippa, Mangham of New Castle, DeVenzio and Wuycik of Ambridge, the Saul brothers of Butler...

Go ahead and pick your guys... tell your stories.

Bob and Jennifer... 1986, 1987, 1988

My next stop in this fantastic Farrell time travel advances me to the 1980's. the destination... well, here it is.

Dateline: Shippensburg University, Seth Grove Stadium – PIAA Track and Field Championship

On three separate occasions Farrell Steeler Track and Field athletes won multiple gold medals in the PIAA championship meet. On May 24, 1986, sophomore Jennifer Sims earned her place at the top of the podium after winning both the 400-meter dash (57.50) and then the 200-meter dash (26.62). On that same day the boys turned a speedy 43.10 in the 4x100 relay to garner Farrell's third gold of the day.

In 1987, May 23 was Bob Samuels Day. The junior won a rare triple in the 100 meters (10.86), 200 meters (22.26), and the 400 meters (48.48). His 100-meter race brought the stadium crowd to its feet as he defeated Raqhib Ismail of Elmer L. Meyers High School by .25 of a second. Of course, Ismail would later gain fame at Notre Dame as "the Rocket."

The most significant day in Farrell Track and Field history was May 28, 1988. Senior Bob Samuels sprinted to his fourth career gold medal in the 400 meters (48.48) and then added his fifth at 200 meters (21.84). He owned his three races during his junior and senior year – five gold and one silver.

110

But this day was for the girls. It was a perfect day, sunny and 86 degrees. It would prove to be a perfectly sunny day for the Steeler ladies. In just the second event of the day, Junior Yvonne McKeithan turned in a time of 15.88 in the 100-meter hurdles for a fourth-place finish and five team points.

The smoke from the starter's pistol had barely dissipated when senior Pam Bacon clocked a 13 flat in the 100 to finish fifth and add four more points to the team total. Two races later senior Jennifer Sims added to her gold medal collection with a 57.18 400-meters. Team total now stood at 18 points.

In the very next race Sims came back to anchor the 4x100 relay. Their gold medal time was 48.44. Then in the ninth race of the day, Sims added a silver medal in the 200 meters, her 25.64 just 0.7 seconds behind the winner. Her day culminated with 28 points for the team. Team total stood at 37 and that would be enough.

The blue and gold girls of Farrell were all gold – the City of Champions 18th state championship.

Back – to – Back... 1995, 1996
Five Weeks in November and December

The last Farrell sports fantasy (and I know, this could go on for a long time) takes me back to the back-to-back state football championship runs of 1995 and 1996. Coach Falconi's squad snapped Southern Columbia's 31 game winning streak to win the championship 6-0 in 1995.

The venerable writer Ray Swanson quoted the Southern Columbia coach in his Keystone column in the *Sharon Herald*, on

December 17, 1995, he said, "We knew Farrell was fast, but they were much more physical than we expected."

Thirty years later, that still fits... Farrell football FAST and PHYSICAL.

The next year, 1996... same site, same opponent, same stakes, same outcome... Farrell – 14, Southern Columbia – 12.

Back-to-Back... here is the data. Enjoy it again, especially the cliffhangers.

1995 WPIAL Victories:

South Fayette 7-0
Western Beaver 25-0
Monessen 30-14

PIAA Victories:

Smethport 14-0   Western Final
Southern Columbia 6-0   State Championship

• Averaged 16.4 points/game
• Allowed 2.8 points/game
• Four shutouts in five games
• 14-1 record
• Amp Pegues QB
• Stan Kennedy TB
• Ben Mercurio NG

1996 WPIAL Victories:

Duquesne 14-0
South Fayette 14-12
Riverview 26-25 (2 OT)

PIAA Victories:

Moshannon Valley 14-10   Western Final
Southern Columbia 14-12   State Championship

• Last four playoff games won by a total of nine points
• 13-1 record
• Carlos Daniels TB
• Dante "Bucky" Newell OL-DL
• Chico Pinkins HB

Chapter Nine

Farrell High School Sports History

Football

• Championships

• Season records 1918 – 2019

• All State Recognition

• Farrell Steelers in professional football

PIAA Football Championship History
PIAA State Champions

1995	1A	Farrell – 6	Southern Columbia – 0 Mansion Park, Altoona
1996	1A	Farrell – 14	Southern Columbia – 12 Mansion Park, Altoona
2018	1A	Farrell – 55	Lackawanna Trail – 20 Hersheypark Stadium
2019	1A	Farrell – 10	Bishop Guilfoyle – 7 Hersheypark Stadium

PIAA State Runners-Up

1990	1A	Marian Catholic –21	Farrell – 13 Memorial Stadium, Middletown
2015	1A	Bishop Guilfoyle – 35	Farrell – 0 Hersheypark Stadium

WPIAL Champions (District 7)

1951	3A
1976	2A
1986	1A
1990	1A
1995	1A
1996	1A

District 10 Champions

1985	Div III	Farrell – 50	Kennedy Christian – 8
2008	A	Farrell – 28	Linesville – 7
2009	A	Farrell – 34	Sharpsville – 7
2010	A	Farrell – 39	Mercyhurst Prep – 0
2015	A	Farrell – 26	Sharpsville – 20 (OT)
2016	A	Farrell – 22	West Middlesex – 12
2017	A	Farrell – 52	Cambridge Springs – 27
2018	A	Farrell – 50	West Middlesex – 6

Football Season Records
1918 – 2019

Season	Record	Season	Record	Season	Record
1918	2-1-0	1952	5-4-0	1987	8-2-0
1919	No team	1953	2-6-1	1988	10-3-0
1920	2-2-0	1954	1-8-1	1989	10-1-1
1921	3-8-0	1955	7-3-0	1990	14-1-0
1922	4-5-0	1956	9-1-0	1991	10-2-0
1923	0-7-1	1957	6-3-0	1992	6-4-0
1924	1-4-0	1958	9-1-0	1993	6-5-0
1925	1-3-0	1959	8-0-2	1994	6-4-0
1926	4-1-3	1960	5-4-1	1995	14-1-0
1927	3-3-2	1961	6-4-0	1996	13-1-0
1928	2-4-3	1962	4-5-1	1997	9-3-0
1929	3-4-0	1963	3-7-0	1998	8-4-0
1930	7-1-0	1964	0-9-1	1999	5-6-0
1931	5-2-2	1965	6-4-0	2000	7-4-0
1932	5-3-1	1966	6-3-1	2001	9-3-0
1933	1-7-0	1967	4-6-0	2002	6-4-0
1934	5-3-2	1968	7-3-0	2003	4-4-1
1935	3-6-0	1969	9-1-0	2004	8-3-0
1936	2-7-1	1970	2-6-2	2005	5-5-0
1937	4-3-1	1971	7-3-0	2006	1-9-0
1938	0-9-0	1972	3-6-1	2007	9-3-0
1939	3-1-0	1973	4-4-1	2008	12-3-0
1940	9-0-0	1974	1-7-1	2009	14-1-0
1941	2-3-3	1975	6-3-0	2010	13-2-0
1942	6-3-0	1976	11-2-0	2011	6-5-0
1943	6-2-0	1978	4-6-0	2012	6-5-0
1944	5-4-1	1979	2-8-0	2013	4-5-0
1945	3-4-2	1980	9-3-0	2014	8-4-0
1946	3-6-1	1981	6-2-2	2015	14-2-0
1947	2-3-4	1982	3-6-0	2016	10-4-0
1948	7-2-0	1983	9-1-1	2017	11-3-0
1949	5-3-1	1984	4-6-0	2018	15-0-0
1950	6-3-0	1985	9-3-0	2019	14-2-0
1951	9-1-0	1986	11-1-1		

Summary: 625-372-44   Compiled by Lou Falconi, Sr.

Post 2019 Addendum

2020	5-3	District 10 Runner-up to Wilmington
2021	11-1	District 10 Champions – Farrell – 48, Wilmington – 0
2022	11-1	District 10 Champions – Farrell – 36, Sharpsville – 0
2023	11-2	District 10 Champions – Farrell – 16, Mercyhurst Prep – 9

Summary: 663-379-44

All-State Football
1940 – 2010

1940	Hugh McKinnis	AP
1959	Brian Generalovich	AP
1960	Brian Generalovich	UPI
1969	Randy Crowder	AP, UPI
1976	Brian Sanders	AP, UPI
1987	Bobby Samuels	AP
1990	Tim Scarvel	AP
1990	Billy Altman	AP
1990	Toby Thomas	AP
1991	Joe Roqueplot	AP
1991	Lorenzo Styles	AP
1995	Stan Kennedy	AP
1996	Carlos Daniels	AP
1997	Jason Kennedy	AP
2008	Terry Perfilio	PA Sportswriters
2009	Danny Odem	PA Sportswriters
2010	Robert Trudo	PA Sportswriters

Farrell Steelers – Professional Football
National Football League

• Tony Paulekas – Center/Linebacker – Packers 1936
(Washington and Jefferson College)
• Pete Hall – End – Giants 1961
(Marquette University)
• Hugh McKinnis – Fullback – Browns/Seahawks 1973-76
(Arizona State University)
• Randy Crowder – Defensive Line – Dolphins/Buccaneers
1974- 80
(Penn State University)
• Judson Flint – Defensive Back – Browns/Bills 1980-83
(California University PA/ Memphis State University)
• Lorenzo Styles – Linebacker – Falcons/Rams 1995-2000 (The
Ohio State University)

Canadian Football League

• Hugh McKinnis – Calgary / Ottawa/British Columbia
• Bob Pegues – Hamilton
• Henry Newby – British Columbia / Calgary / Montreal /
Winnipeg / Saskatchewan

Girls Volleyball
PIAA State Champions

1982	2A
1987	2A
1989	2A
1993	2A
1994	2A
1998	2A
2001	1A
2002	1A

PIAA State Runners-Up

1983	2A
1992	2A
1997	2A
2000	1A
2003	1A

WPIAL Championships (District 7)

1981	2A
1982	2A
1983	2A
1984	2A
1985	2A
1986	2A
1987	2A
1989	2A
1990	2A
1992	2A
1993	2A
1994	2A
1995	2A
1996	2A

1999	2A
2000	1A
2001	1A
2002	1A
2003	1A
2004	1A

Coach Harriett Morrison
554-59 (Farrell record)
22 consecutive PIAA playoff appearances
5 undefeated seasons

Boys Basketball

PIAA State Champions

1952	3A
1954	3A
1956	3A
1959	3A
1960	3A
1969	3A
1972	3A

Note: In 1952 the Farrell Steelers arrived in Philadelphia via a chartered United States Army cargo plane.

PIAA State Runners-up

1943	3A
1951	3A
2015	1A

WPIAL Champions (District 7)

1951	3A
1952	3A
1954	3A
1956	3A
1959	3A
1960	3A
1969	3A
1971	3A
1972	3A
1974	3A
1976	3A
1984	4A
1992	4A

District 10 Championships

1931
1938
1940
1943
2009
2014

All-State Basketball

Henry Thomas	1938
Steve Skendrovich	1943
Julius McCoy	1951, 1952
Jimmy McCoy	1954
Don Jones	1956
Pete Hall	1956
Brian Generalovich	1960
Willie Somerset	1960
Jack Marin	1962
Dave Johnson	1962
Larry Prince	1972
Danny Stewart	1972
Marsell Holden	2009
Malik Miller	2015, 2016

Coach Ed McCluskey
590-153 (Farrell record)

Basketball – NBA, ABA

• Jack Marin – Guard/Forward – Bullets/Rockets/Braves/Bulls – 1966-77 (Duke University)
• Willie Somerset – Guard – Bullets/Mavericks/Nets – 1965-69 (Duquesne University)

Basketball State Champions

1952 AAA	Farrell 63	Coatesville 55	Palestra, Philadelphia
1954 AAA	Farrell 63	Chester 52	Palestra, Philadelphia
1956 AAA	Farrell 57	Palmerton 45	Palestra, Philadelphia
1959 AAA	Farrell 76	Chester 66	Palestra, Philadelphia
1960 AAA	Farrell 61	Radnor 40	Farm Show Arena, Harrisburg
1969 AAA	Farrell 61	Steelton-Highspire 50	Farm Show Arena, Harrisburg
1972 AAA	Farrell 56	Chester 55	Farm Show Arena, Harrisburg

Wrestling
PIAA State Champions (Team)

1945
1946
1949

PIAA State Champions (Individuals)

1944	George Lewis	95
1944	Howdy Prizant	112
1945	George Lewis	103
1945	John Bralich	165
1946	George Lewis	112
1946	Achilles Mouganis	145
1947	Vic DeVito	133
1949	Tom Springer	120

1950 was the last year of the wrestling program.

Girls Track and Field
1988 PIAA State Champions (Team)
PIAA State Champions (Individuals)

1980	AA	4x100 Relay		49.18
1986	AA	Jennifer Sims	400	57.50
1986	AA	Jennifer Sims	200	26.62
1988	AA	4x100 Relay		49.44
1988	AA	Jennifer Sims	400	57.18
1990	AA	Tiffany Goudy	Triple Jump	39-9 3/4

Boys Track and Field
1987 PIAA State Runner-Up (Team)
PIAA State Champions (Individuals)

1996	A	Adrian Capitol	100-yard dash	10.1
1997	A	Adrian Capitol	220-yard dash	20.8
1986	AA	4x100 Relay		43.10
1987	AA	Bob Samuels	400	48.48
1987	AA	Bob Samuels	200	22.26
1987	AA	Bob Samuels	100	10.86
1988	AA	Bob Samuels	400	49.49
1988	AA	Bob Samuels	200	21.94
1991	AA	4x400 Relay		3:23.41

Boys Volleyball
1986 State Runner-up (Team)

All Sports Championship Summary

Farrell Steelers All Sports Championship Summary

	State Champions	State Runners Up	District Champions
Girls Volleyball	8	5	20
Boys Basketball	7	3	19
Football	4	2	16
Wrestling	3		
Girls Track and Field	1		
Boys volleyball		1	2
Boys Track and Field		1	1
Girls Basketball			3

All Sports Championship Summary
(23) State Championships:

(8) Girls Volleyball	1982,1987,1989,1993,1994,1998,2001,2002
(7) Boys Basketball	1952,1954,1956,1959,1960,1969,1972
(4) Football	1995,1996,2018,2019
(3) Wrestling	1945,1946,1949
(1) Girls Track and Field	1988

(12) State Runners Up:

(5) Girls Volleyball	1983,1992,1997,2000,2003
(3) Boys Basketball	1943,1951,2015
(2) Football	1990,2015
(1) Boys Track and Field	1987
(1) Boys Volleyball	1986

(44) WPIAL (District 7) Champions:

(20) Girls Volleyball	
(13) Boys Basketball	
(6) Football	1951,1976,1986,1990,1995,1996
(2) Boys Volleyball	1986,1992
(2) Girls Track and Field	1985,1992
(1) Boys Track and Field	1982

(19) District 10 Champions:

(10) Football	1942,1985,2008,2009,2010,2015,2016,2017,2018,2019
(6) Boys Basketball	1931,1938,1940,1943,2009,2014
(3) Girls Basketball	2007,2008,2010

Epilogue
Repeat... 2019 State Champions

PIAA State Playoffs

"No way, I'll never kick a field goal!" (Amp)

Epilogue

Repeat… 2019 State Champions

PIAA State Playoffs

Farrell 60 – Tussey Mountain 14

Farrell 28 – Coudersport 0

Farrell 13 – Clairton 10

Farrell 10 – Bishop Guilfoyle 7

Following the 2019 championship and Coach Samuels' retirement, Amp Pegues assumed the dual roles of head football coach and athletic director. He immediately proved he could wear both hats well. Amp would continue to direct the offense which would average 36.5 points per game in the championship season. The defense coordinated by Omar Stewart, Sr. allowed only 7 points per game. The Steel Curtain registered an incredible nine shutouts. It could be said that Amp's cool was balanced by Omar's fire.

The biggest obstacle on the road to the championship game was the Steelers' long-time nemesis perennial power, Clairton. The nail-biting 13-10 Western Final win was a testament to the stout defense prepared by coaches Stewart, Bucky Newell, and Lamont Samuels. The defensive effort featured eight sacks by defensive ends Sayvion Thomas and Brian Hilton, Jr. and three interceptions by Amarion Odem (2) and Brice Butler (1).

In the four PIAA playoff games Farrell outgained their opponents an average of 289 to 163 total yards. Anthony Stallworth led the offense with 130 rushing yards per game. The offensive attack was significantly a ground attack averaging only 37 passing yards per game.

The Fantastic Finish

The senior group of Raver, Hilton, Daniels, Hobson, Hopson, Thomas, Hammonds, Ravenscraft, Tarver, Burris, and Samuels were just eighth graders in 2015 when Bishop Guilfoyle clobbered Farrell 35-0 in the state championship game. Many of the current coaching staff were on the sidelines on that day in 2015. They remembered that game.

Farrell entered the game anchored by their strength at the line of scrimmage. "Heart and Soul" was expertly coached by Victor Phillips. The line included: Gary Hopson, Jr., Melvin Hobson, Jr., Gary Satterwhite III, Preston Williams, and Adrien Daniels.
Football games are won at the line of scrimmage. This formidable group averaged 292 pounds and was critical in the Steelers' Championship season.

On the season, Farrell outscored their fifteen opponents 539 to 98 and outgained them 5,180 yards to 2,438 yards.
Stallworth entered the championship game with 1,656 rushing yards and Harrison added 984. Butler had 19 receptions, Hilton 20, and Harrison 15.

A Field Goal!

Amp's brother Marlon had once told him, "At some point in time, you're gonna have to kick a field goal."

To which Amp thought, "No way, I'll never kick a field goal!"

Coach Falconi thought that never in a million years would he have believed that a field goal would be the difference. Considering the cold and windy conditions on this day, Lou said "I was dyin'… I hope we don't try this."

More on that later.

The game was largely a stalemate, although the Steelers outgained the Marauders 215-103. The scoring drives were indicative of the slugfest. Farrell scored in the second quarter on a 21 yard "drive" after a Guilfoyle fumble. Raver scored on a one-yard QB sneak.

Then Guilfoyle scored in fourth quarter on a three play five yard "drive" after blocking a Farrell punt. Myrick scored from the one-yard line.

So, the two teams combined for 26 yards of touchdown "drives" each culminating with one yard touchdown runs.

Football History is Made

The scoreboard read 7-7 after 48 minutes. Football history was just moments away. In the long history of football, there have been hundreds of thousands of games played. It is unlikely that what occurred next had ever happened before.

No Hollywood screenwriter would write this because of its ridiculous implausibility. Let's just put it in overtime…and make it a State Championship game.

On the fourth play of overtime, Brian Hilton, Jr. slashed in from the left edge into the critical area in front of Wyandt's field goal attempt. Parallel to the ground, in an all-out diving effort, he blocked the kick. An incredible play!

But that's not enough drama. It is necessary to go back to third down. Savvy safety Brice Butler made the first brilliant play of overtime. He executed a perfect read as Myrick attempted a deceptive Tim Tebow-like jump pass. Brice made a touchdown saving stop, batting down the pass. That play, perhaps overlooked by the casual fan, set up Brian's brilliant block.

Now, back to the ridiculously implausible Hollywood script:

Farrell then took their turn on offense in overtime. Unable to score on three plays… next came the most unlikely decision in Steeler history. Amp called for a field goal, the call he was never going to make!

Let's add some more drama. The kicker will be Brian Hilton, Jr. who had never attempted a field goal. And yes, that is the same guy that just moments ago blocked Guilfoyle's field goal attempt.

Just for kicks, let's direct a stiff wind into the kicker's face. The tension was thicker than Hershey hot fudge!

The snap... the hold... the kick. It caught the wind and went seemingly straight up into the air... And then... miraculously it dropped straight down inches over the cross bar!

Farrell 10 – Bishop Guilfoyle 7

Hollywood ... how's that??

- State Championship game goes into overtime
- Kid blocks opponent's field goal attempt
- Coach who never calls for a field goal – calls for a field goal
- Same kid who has never attempted a field goal – attempts a field goal
- Remember... it's only overtime in the State Championship game
- Stiff wind catches the kick... it miraculously drops straight down just inches over the cross bar

Coach Pegues' who had experienced such great success as a player and as an assistant coach was now a state champion coach in his debut season.

Amp humbly deflected the praise directed toward him... "This is all about the kids. Puttin' in the time and the effort and gettin' it done. It's always about them."

By The Numbers

Farrell		Guilfoyle
11	First Downs	7
201	Rushing Yards	72
14	Passing Yards	31
8-2-0	Att-Comp-Int.	6-2-1
215	Total Yards	103
3-1	Fumbles/Lost	3-2
11-82	Penalties/Yards	6-30
Farrell	0 – 7 – 0- -0 – 3…10	
Bishop Guilfoyle	0 – 0 – 0 – 7 – 0…7	

2019 Season Results

8-23	USO	12-14
8-30	@ Wilmington	0-40
9-6	Union City	35-0
9-13	West Middlesex	33-0
9-20	@ Cambridge Springs	63-0
9-27	@ Mercer	73-0
10-4	Cochranton	54-0
10-11	Reynolds	51-0
10-18	@ Greenville	39-0
10-25	Cambridge Springs	2-0 forfeit
11-1	West Middlesex	42-0
11-8 **District 10 Championship Game**	Maplewood @ Meadville	35-20
11-16 **PIAA Round of 16**	Tussey Mountain @ SRU	60-14
11-22 **PIAA Quarterfinals**	Coudersport @ Dubois	28-0
11-29 **Western Final**	Clairton @ North Allegheny	13-10
12-5 **State Championship**	Bishop Guilfoyle @ Hersheypark	10-7 (OT)

2019 Roster

1 – Anthony Jackson	SO, 5-9, 185	RB/SS
2 – Christian Hartley	JR, 5-9, 205	QB/RB
3 – Anthony Stallworth	SO, 5-11, 185	RB/LB
5 – Omar Stewart, Jr.	SO, 6-1, 160	WR/DB
6 – Ray Raver, Jr.	SR, 5-10, 175	QB/DB
7 – Brice Butler	JR, 5-10, 170	WR/DB
8 – Taidon Strickland	SO, 5-10, 190	RB/LB
9 – Jaden Harrison	JR, 5-10, 150	RB/DB
10 – Lamont Samuels	FR, 5-5, 125	QB/WR/DB
11 – Josiah Tarver	SR, 6-1, 185	WR/DB
12 – Brian Hilton, Jr.	SR, 6-2, 175	WR/DE/K/P
13 – Zion Scarbrough	FR, 5-5, 120	WR/DB
14 – Denzel Driver	SO, 6-3, 170	WR/DB
15 – Amarion Odem	JR, 6-1, 175	WR/DB
16 – Jermaine Jackson	FR, 5-10, 150	WR/DB
17 – Javon Bell	FR, 5-2, 120	WR/DB
19 – Ja'Sean Boatwright	FR, 6-0, 175	WR/DB
20 – Tyrie Hammonds	SR, 5-8, 160	RB/LB
21 – Herold Hooten, Jr.	FR, 5-9, 130	WR/DB
22 – Kien Wade	FR, 6-1, 165	WR/DB
23 – Tahjmere Gibson	FR, 5-3, 145	RB/LB
24 – Juwon Samuels	SR, 5-9, 170	WR/DB
25 – Kylon Wilson	FR, 5-5, 130	RB/DB
26 – Sayvion Thomas	SR, 5-11, 170	RB/DE
27 – Josiah West	SO, 5-7, 130	WR/DB
40 – TiMarr Lacamera	FR, 5-5, 140	LB
51 – Allen Jackson	SO, 6-1, 250	OL/DL
52 – Dwight Ravenscraft	SR, 5-8, 185	OL/LB
53 – Anthony Jackson	FR, 6-4, 260	OL/DL
54 – Gary Satterwhite, III	JR, 6-2, 295	OL/DL
56 – Preston Williams	SO, 6-0, 350	OL/DL
57 – Ondre Burris	SR, 6-4, 390	OL/DL
58 – Malachi Shepherd	FR, 6-0, 200	OL/DL
60 – Cameron Burris	JR, 6-0, 350	OL/DL
64 – Jeremiah Butler	JR, 6-2, 170	OL/DL
66 – Gary Hopson, Jr.	SR, 5-11, 282	OL/DL
70 – Adrian Daniels	SR, 6-4, 230	TE/DE
75 – Melvin Hobson, Jr.	SR, 6-4, 305	OL/DL

2019 Coaching Staff

Amp Pegues
Omar Stewart
Victor Phillips
Bucky Newell
Kurt Chester
Emil Debonis
Lamont Samuels
Troy Harrison
Brian Hilton, Sr.
Robert Townsend
Darwin Dixon
Jason Marshall
Warren Robinson
Dontell Morgan
Sam Phillips
Marquis Samuels
Lou Falconi

2019 Post Season Honors

District 10 – Region 1 All Stars

First Team Offense
QB Raver
RB Stallworth
AP Harrison
WR Butler
WR Hilton, Jr.
OL Hobson, Jr.
OL Satterwhite III
OL Hopson, Jr.
K Hilton, Jr.

Second Team Offense
OL Daniels

First Team Defense
DL Hobson, Jr.
DL Hopson, Jr.
DL Daniels
DL Thomas
LB Hammonds
LB Strickland
LB Ravenscraft
LB Jackson
DB Samuels
DB Raver
DB Butler

Second Team Defense
DL Hilton, Jr.
DB Odem
P Hilton, Jr.

2019 Pennsylvania Football Writers All-State Team

Offense
QB Raver
RB Stallworth
OL Satterwhite III

Defense
DL Hilton, Jr.
Hobson, Jr.
LB Thomas
LB Strickland
DB Butler

Coach of the Year
Amp Pegues

Acknowledgements

Over the last several years I have had many conversations about the Farrell community, Farrell football, and the tradition of Farrell sports.

I am particularly grateful to my friend and former linebacker, Jarrett Samuels who allowed me an insider's view of the juggernaut that he guided for ten years.

The numerous sideline conversations on the practice field with Lou Falconi were always colorful, helpful, and informative.

My dear friend, the late Janet Shannon, secretary of the Farrell class of 1957, provided invaluable information about the city, the school, and Steeler sports.

Here follows a somewhat comprehensive list of people with whom I had conversations. Most are graduates of Farrell High School. They were probably not aware but they were adding depth and texture, color and insight into this story. To all of them, I am thankful.

Jarrett Samuels '91, Lou Falconi '65, Janet Chisholm Shannon '57, Stan Shannon, Amp Pegues '96, Omar Stewart '91, Tracey Samuels, Gary Swanson, Kobe Hilton '19, Christian Lewis '19, Jourdan Townsend '19, Kyi Wright '19, Superintendent Lora Adams-King '82, Bucky Newell '97, Troy Harrison '79, Principal Matt Fowler '98, Assistant Principal Brian Vecchia, Riley Smoot '75, Emil DeBonis '76, Jennifer Sims '91, Brandon Lewis '92, Fred DeBonis '52, Trainer Dan Braatz, Athletic Director Dan Dragicevic, Assistant AD Jim Cardamon, Video crew Colleen De' Angelo, Louis Berry Jr., Brandon Phillian, JR McFarland, Harry Zehnder, Tom Ritchey.

Special thanks to Mark Slezak and Ralph Blundo for their thoughtful Foreword words. And to Olivia Fulkerson for her typing assistance. And to Ginger and Brian at Westminster College for their kindness.

Finally, I would be remiss to not acknowledge the excellent comprehensive coverage of local high school sports by the *Sharon Herald's* Ed Farrell. The Steelers provided exciting stories and Ed's reportage was superb.

And, a sentimental thanks to the late former *Herald* and *Vindicator* sportswriter, Ray Swanson. My friend, Gary Swanson, permitted me access to Ray's archives which fueled my enthusiasm for this project.

You would not have had a book to read without the considerable patience, steadfast encouragement, and publishing acumen of Juliann Mangino of Doc Publishing.

And finally, finally…thanks to my family that blesses me daily…my wife, Sally, and daughters, Bethany and Rachel, and their families, whose support in this and all matters causes my cup to overflow with gratitude.

About the Author

Darwin Huey was a professor of Education at Westminster College, PA for 41 years. He has also served as an Assistant Football Coach/Defensive Coordinator (23 years), Chair of the Department of Education (13 years), Director of the Graduate Program (12 years), and Director of Audio-Visual Services (12 years). Darwin Huey is also the author of *Together: The Inside Story of the 2014 New Castle Red Hurricane Pennsylvania State AAAA Basketball Championship.*

He holds bachelor's and master's degrees from Westminster and a doctorate from the University of Pittsburgh.

His most important titles are husband to Sally; Daddy to Bethany and Rachel; Poppy to Gemma Adair, Selah Grace, Willa Lillian, and Amayah Rae (Pip); and father-in-law to Marcus and Nathan.

You can contact the author at hueydw@westminster.edu.

Post-game locker room...pictured are Christian Lewis, after his five-touchdown game, Coach-of-the-Year, Jarrett Samuels with the State Championship trophy, and Darwin Huey, the author.

Sources

Sharon Herald...Stories by Sportswriter Ed Farrell.

"Farrell's Fabled Football Program Adds Another Chapter with 2015 Edition", December 14, 2015.

"Exorcising Past Demons", September 1, 2018.

"Steelers Senior Speedster Lewis Leads Steelers to 40-0 Region Win", September 15, 2018.

"Farrell Eyes State Title: Steelers Have Added Incentive vs. Lackawanna Trail", December 5, 2018.

"Farrell Rolls to 55-20 Win to Become Mercer County First Undefeated State Champion", December 7, 2018.

"Farrell's Fabled Football Season Ends with Samuels, Wright and Five Others Cited by State's Sportswriters", December 29, 2018.

"Hilton's Hang Time Gets the Gold for the Steelers", December 6, 2019

"Seniors Lead the Way to Victory", December 7, 2019.

Other Sources

Axelrod, Phil. "Julius McCoy: Basketball Star in 50's at Farrell High School", *Pittsburgh Post-Gazette,* April 11, 2008.

Barksdale-Hall, Roland. *Images of America: African Americans in Mercer County.* Chicago: Arcadia Press, 2009.

Barksdale-Hall, Roland. *Images of America: Farrell.* Chicago: Arcadia Press, 2012.

Cherry, Robert. *Wilt-Larger than Life.* Chicago: Triumph Books, 2004.

Cmor, Philip. "Steelers Cruise in PIAA Opener with 56-8 Victory", *CNHI News Service.*

Ellsworth, Scott. *The Secret Game.* New York: Little Brown and Company, 2015.

Farabaugh, Pat. *An Unbreakable Bond.* Haworth, NJ: St. Johann Press, 2014.

Frketic, Josh. *"Fearsome Foursome: Farrell Eyes Deep Run in 2018",* *WYTV.com,* August 14, 2018.

Jones, Don. *The Path Set Before Me.* Hermitage, PA: Green Street Press, 2008.

Kriegal, Mark. *Namath: A Biography.* New York: Penguin Group USA, 2004.

"Legend Dies: Former Farrell Star McCoy Dies at 76", April 11, 2008. *www.nccnewsonline.com.*

Lenzmeier, Trevor. "Farrell: Community Still Proud of Athletic, Industrial Past…Tries to Build Future", *Pittsburgh Post-Gazette,* November *10, 2018.*

Pedasfamily.com. History of Farrell, Pennsylvania: 1901-2001.

Pepe, Johnny. "Sports Sauce", *Sharon Herald, December 29, 1954.*

Raykie, Jim. "Death of Pittsburgh Hoops Star Conjures Up Memories", *Sharon Herald,* March 1, 2008.

Swanson, Ray. "Farrell 6 – Southern Columbia 0…State Champions", *Sharon Herald,* December 17, 1995.

Swanson, Ray. Archival files from the *Sharon Herald (Keystone Corner)* and the *Youngstown Vindicator (Keystoner).*

Vosburg, Bob. *Scooter's Days and Other Days.* New Wilmington, PA: New Horizons Publishing, 1997.

Vosburg, Bob. *This Man's Castle.* New Wilmington, PA: New Horizons Publishing, 2005.

Wilkerson, Isabel. *The Warmth of Other Suns.* New York: Vintage Books, 2010.